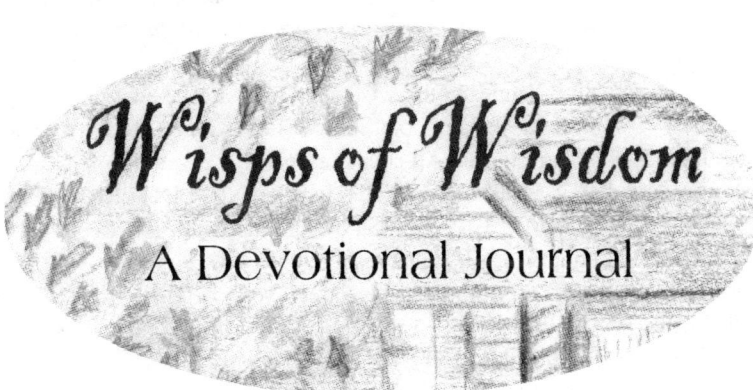

Wisps of Wisdom
A Devotional Journal

Carol Fitchhorn

Belleville, Ontario, Canada

Wisps of Wisdom
Copyright © 2007, Carol Fitchhorn
All Rights Reserved. No part of this publication may be reproduced, stored in a retrieval system or transmitted in any form or by any means—electronic, mechanical, photocopy, recording or any other—except for brief quotations in printed reviews, without the prior permission of the author.

All Scripture quotations, unless otherwise specified, are taken from the New King James Version of the Bible. Copyright © 1979, 1980, 1982 by Thomas Nelson, Inc. Used by permission. All rights reserved.
Scriptures marked NIV are from the HOLY BIBLE, NEW INTERNATIONAL VERSION. Copyright © 1973, 1978, 1984 by International Bible Society. Used by permission of Zondervan. All rights reserved.
Scriptures marked KJV are from the King James Version of the Bible, GIANT PRINT REFERENCE EDITION. Copyright © 1990 by Thomas Nelson, Inc. Used by permission. All rights reserved.
Cover design sketched by Nadja Fitchhorn Haddon
Library and Archives Canada Cataloguing in Publication
Fitchhorn, Carol, 1950-
   Wisps of wisdom : a devotional journal / Carol Fitchhorn.
ISBN 1-55452-104-1
   1. Devotional calendars. I. Title.
BV4811.F575 2006   242'.2   C2006-905667-6

**For more information or
to order additional copies, please contact:**
Carol Fitchhorn
wisps_of_wisdom@sbcglobal.net

Guardian Books is an imprint of *Essence Publishing,* a Christian Book Publisher dedicated to furthering the work of Christ through the written word. For more information, contact:
20 Hanna Court, Belleville, Ontario, Canada K8P 5J2.
Direct: 613-962-0234 • Toll Free: 1-800-238-6376 • Fax: 613-962-4711.
E-mail: info@essence-publishing.com
Web site: www.essence-publishing.com

Printed in Canada
by
Guardian BOOKS

My earthly journey began in 1950 when God gave me to my parents, Russell and Janet Munyan. Thank you both for your love, biblical instruction, discipline, and encouragement. I have become the woman I am because you taught me to believe in God and because you believed in me.

Daddy, thank you for my name, which means "song of joy." I hope I have been a song of joy in your life.

Mom, you were my first mentor. You practiced what you preached, and you are my Proverbs 31 woman.

There is a bit of each of you in this book. Thank you for training me up in the way I should go; thank you for the wisdom passed on to me over the years. I dedicate this book to you with a heart full of gratitude, and I love you both with all my heart.

Acknowledgments

There are no words that can express the love and thanks I have for the many people God has placed in my life who helped make this book become a reality.

Ken, thank you for your encouragement, your faith in my writing ability, and your financial backing. You have been my best friend and faithful husband during the past forty-four years. God knew I needed you before I did and orchestrated the events in our lives that put us together.

Nadja Haddon and Jimmy Fitchhorn—my beautiful children—thank you for your ideas, creativity, and encouragement to think big. Nadja, I love my book cover—thank you! Most of all, thank you both for the six beautiful grandchildren your dad and I have received through your marriages. Breah, Jessy, Zoë, Devyn, Darian, and Lauren, you are truly the jewels in my crown.

Ben Randall—senior pastor at New Hope Christian Fellowship, Vacaville, California—your sermons from God's Word have inspired many of these devotions. Thank you for not compromising the truth as you lead your sheep.

Donna Stephens—my pastor, mentor, boss, and friend—you planted the seed for this book and gave me gentle nudges along the way. You saw something in me that I did not see in myself. Thank you for encouraging me to keep writing.

Phyllis Seminoff—my dear friend—God placed you in my life for such a time as this. Thank you for the hours spent reading, editing, and brainstorming with me over the past several years. This book is as much yours as it is mine. We are truly soul mates who love the gift of writing. The best is yet to come!

Stephanie Parrish, God knew I needed some constructive criticism from a professional editor, and I believe He sent you to New Hope just for

me! I have incorporated some of your suggestions in *Wisps of Wisdom*. May God bless you and your business, Wise Words Editing, as you continue to influence words for Him.

Sherrill Brunton—my project editor—thank you and the staff at Essence Publishing for making this project a pleasant experience. I love the finished product.

Nancy Minion, thank you for reading part of my manuscript and giving me creative ideas for my title. You felt strongly that the word wisdom needed to be included in the title; I believe God agreed and gave my "wisps" of devotions a name.

To all of my family and friends who have contributed to some of the principles I share in this book, thank you. You know who you are, and I love you dearly. It is my prayer that you will find the satisfaction and fulfillment in life that I have found by obeying God and completing this work.

Author's Preface

Wisps of Wisdom did not begin as a book. I began writing these short daily devotions in 1999 for my church's Web site. After reading the devotions for several weeks, Donna Stephens, our women's ministries' pastor, wrote me a short note: "Are you keeping a diary of these? May become a devotional book someday—thought about it?" At that moment the seed was sown, and I began the journey of writing this book. It has been a seven-year project with many detours; but each time I became sidetracked, God has been faithful to draw me back.

As I considered how to arrange these devotions, I felt in my heart that God wanted me to present them to you in the same way He gave them to me—day by day, flowing with the movement of the Holy Spirit as He directed me through the Word. Sometimes the devotions are connected with a common theme over several days; other times the topic changes daily. At the end of each short prayer I have placed an ellipsis. It is my desire that you will continue that prayer using your own words, jotting down what God is speaking to you at that moment.

I pray that these wisps of wisdom are an encouragement to you, as they have been to me. May God bless you on your journey with Him.

*Oh, the depth of the riches both of the
wisdom and knowledge of God!*
—Romans 11:33

January

January 1

New Beginnings

So he answered and said to me: "This is the word of the LORD to Zerubbabel: 'Not by might nor by power, but by My Spirit,' says the LORD of hosts."

—Zechariah 4:6

It is New Year's Day as I write this: a new year—a new beginning—a time to resolve to do those things that will make me a better person. As I reflect on my past resolutions to become better, I know that I cannot do it on my own.

This year God has planted a desire within me to organize my time and possessions. In His goodness, He reminds me that I don't have to do it alone. He has given me (and every believer) the Holy Spirit as my Helper. It is only through the Spirit that I will be able to keep my resolution to become more organized.

I know that when God places a life change on your heart, He will provide you with the resources to accomplish it. Ask Him to help you keep whatever resolutions you have made for the new year. You can trust Him to help you do all He has called you to do.

Prayer

Lord, I have a huge task before me this year. Thank You for promising to help me get it done. I place my heart and my resolution in Your hands…

_____

_____

_____

_____

_____

_____

_____

January 2

Ordered Gardens

Let all things be done decently and in order.

—1 Corinthians 14:40

Recently I borrowed a friend's copy of *Ordering Your Private World* by Gordon MacDonald. As I was reading the book one morning, the following sentence stood out: "God does not often walk in disordered gardens."[1] MacDonald was talking about our inner selves: our thoughts, our goals, and our priorities. I was seeing my outer self: piles of mail, Christmas wrap and gifts that needed to be cleared away, books I had shelved to read at a later date, closets that needed to be organized, things that needed to go to Good Will, and a book I was writing that needed to be finished. I began to realize that God wants order in every area—inside and out.

How do we bring order into our day? By scheduling quiet time with the Lord. When we begin our day with Him, God will then bring order into every area of our lives—inside and out. As we begin to prioritize and organize, things will fall into place, and God will be able to walk with us in our ordered gardens.

Prayer

Heavenly Father, You created this world with order for a purpose. Please help me to organize my world for Your purpose…

January 3

Be Still

Be still, and know that I am God; I will be exalted among the nations, I will be exalted in the earth!

—Psalm 46:10

In a busy, computerized, twenty-four-hour-a-day society, does anyone really know what being still means? God calls us to stop—really stop—and know Him. He wants us to pause and get to know Him as we listen to the birds; touch a fragrant, delicate petal on a flower; feel a soft breeze as it caresses our face or inhale the freshness of the rain-moistened earth. He wants us to see Him as we watch a breathtaking sunset or walk on the beach, knowing that His hand separates the water from the sand. God wants us to know Him through His written Word, as we sit quietly and wait to hear His voice as He speaks to us.

God speaks to you in everything that surrounds you. Can you hear His voice? Or are you too busy with life's distractions to be still and hear Him? Close your eyes for a moment, forget your surroundings, and listen; do you hear and feel God all around you? Breathe in deeply and absorb Him into your innermost being. Be still and know that He is God.

Prayer

Father, please help me to put aside my hectic schedule for a short while. Enable me to sit quietly, listen, and hear Your voice—to be still and know that You are my God…

January 4

In God's Hands

Therefore do not worry about tomorrow, for tomorrow will worry about its own things. Sufficient for the day is its own trouble.

—Matthew 6:34

With wars in the world, global-wide famines, the return of old plagues, and an increase in the severity of natural disasters in recent years, who would not be worried? But as believers, God calls us not to be worriers. To be concerned about and prepared for a situation is not the same as worrying. In everything we must remind ourselves that God is in control. He will provide the strength and the supplies for everything He asks us to do.

Do not worry about tomorrow, friend. Put all of your days in God's hands. He is the one who created you and ordained each day of your life. He is in control.

Prayer

Heavenly Father, You are in control of my life. Help me not to worry and to live each day as it is given to me. You are my Strength and my Provider for all of my days…

_____
_____
_____
_____
_____
_____

January 5

Obeying God

So Samuel said: "Has the Lord as great delight in burnt offerings and sacrifices, As in obeying the voice of the Lord? Behold, to obey is better than sacrifice, And to heed than the fat of rams."

—1 Samuel 15:22

Saul was told by God to go in and utterly destroy all of the Amalekites, as well as all of their possessions and animals. But Saul disobeyed God's command. He destroyed only what he felt was vile and unclean and kept all that he felt was good.

When asked by the prophet Samuel why he had not killed all of the animals, Saul rationalized that he spared the best ones for sacrificing to God. Instead of being pleased with Saul's actions, God was angry. He wanted Saul's obedience more than He wanted his sacrifice. As a result of Saul's disobedience to God's command, he lost his kingdom.

What riches are you being stripped of because you are not obeying God's voice?

Prayer

Lord, please forgive me for my disobedience. Help me listen to Your instruction and then obey...

_____

_____

_____

_____

_____

January 6

Built by God

Unless the Lord builds the house, They labor in vain who build it; Unless the Lord guards the city, The watchman stays awake in vain.

—Psalm 127:1

In this psalm, King Solomon recognized that we should live our lives dependent on the Lord. Yet many of us are struggling to build strong homes and churches and forgetting where our true strength lies. We are trying to become super beings and are literally working ourselves to death as we try to do things in our own strength.

While we are busy doing things on our own, our quiet time with the Lord is often neglected. All of our labors and the protection we wish to afford our families are in vain if we neglect to put God first and make Him Lord of our life. God can only be the Builder and Keeper of our homes and churches if we invite Him to take first place in everything.

If you haven't already done so, take time right now to ask God to take His rightful place as the head of your home.

Prayer

Dear Lord, I do not want to labor in vain. I want You to be Lord of my life and the Keeper of my home…

_____

_____

_____

_____

_____

_____

January 7

Encourage One Another

And let us consider one another in order to stir up love and good works, not forsaking the assembling of ourselves together, as is the manner of some, but exhorting one another, and so much the more as you see the Day approaching.

—Hebrews 10:24–25

Many people feel that they can be religious without going to church. But God does not call us to be religious; He calls us to become believers whose faith rests on the crucified and risen Christ. His desire for us as believers is to be a united family until Christ returns. We are to encourage one another until that time.

Is there someone in your church who is sick and needs a meal? Do you know of a young mom you could babysit for who would really appreciate a day away from the kids? Perhaps you know of an elderly person who would enjoy a phone call from anyone. Ask the Lord to reveal to you someone you can encourage today.

Prayer

Thank You, Lord, for giving me my church family. Please help me to always be loving, considerate, and respectful to them. Remind me daily to look for someone to encourage…

January 8

A Gift from God

This is the day the Lord has made; We will rejoice and be glad in it.

—Psalm 118:24

God gives us a beautiful day every day. Each day is beautiful because we are alive and can rejoice in the salvation we have; each day is beautiful because God is in control; each day is beautiful because God will never leave us or forsake us (Hebrews 13:5). We can rejoice because He is our strength in the midst of sickness, heartache, death, depression, financial woes—anything the world can throw at us. Because God made each day, there is always something good to be found in it.

When things are going bad, ask God to show you the good in the situation. Then make the most of your day in spite of the circumstances. Accept each day as a gift from God; live each day as fully as possible!

Prayer

Heavenly Father, thank You for the newness of every day. Help me to live each day in the fullness of You…

January 9

Never Too Young

Let no one despise your youth, but be an example to the believers in word, in conduct, in love, in spirit, in faith, in purity.

—1 Timothy 4:12

Often, as adults, we do not give enough credit to our young people. God can, and does, use them in mighty ways. Timothy was young when he was taken under Paul's wings as a "preacher in training." Because of his youth, he was teachable—not set in his ways—and God used Timothy to help grow the early church.

You may be influencing a young person in your life whom God is going to use in a mighty way. Ask God to help you be an example to this person. Encourage young believers to trust in God and not rely on what they think they can do for Him, but to rely on the empowerment that He can bestow on them.

Prayer

Lord, please help me to always encourage my younger sisters and brothers in Christ to rely on Your strength and not their own. Please help me be a good example to them and give me the ability to look beyond their youth and see the vision You have for their lives…

January 10

Give Them Jesus

Train up a child in the way he should go, and when he is old he will not depart from it.

—Proverbs 22:6

Children in the twenty-first century need God in their lives more than ever before. Satan knows his time is short and is trying every means available to secure his future through our children. Young minds can be easily swayed if not given something or someone to believe in and hold on to. From day one, parents and grandparents need to root their little ones in Jesus. We need to get them into church, sing songs of faith to them and let them hear us read the Bible. Let's provide a good start! God doesn't tell us what happens to our children during those years between childhood and becoming an adult, but He does promise if they are trained in the Word, they will return to Him!

Begin to teach your children about Jesus today. Imprint on their eager minds that He is the way, the truth, and the life (John 14:6). Do not allow Satan to claim the only things in your life that are irreplaceable.

Prayer

Precious Lord, help me to be strong and to ground my children in Your principles. When they seem to be straying, please remind me of Your promise that if I raise them in the way of the Lord they will return…

January 11

Trickled Down

Therefore know that the Lord your God, He is God, the faithful God who keeps covenant and mercy for a thousand generations with those who love Him and keep His commandments.

—Deuteronomy 7:9

The influence of a godly parent or grandparent can affect more than one or two generations. God tells us that "a thousand generations" can reap the rewards afforded to them by the life and prayers of a God-fearing ancestor.

I firmly believe that my maternal great-grandmother was one of my ancestors in the Lord. My mother was partially raised by her grandmother and learned about God while living in her home. I don't know who influenced my great-grandmother, but that influence has trickled down through the generations.

When things get tough and you feel as if the prayers for your loved ones are not being heard or answered, hang in there! Keep those prayers flowing and your influence strong; do not give up! Look beyond the present and into the future; you are impacting your family for years to come.

Prayer

Heavenly Father, my life can affect my family for many generations. When I get discouraged, help me to be strong and live my life daily as an example of Your love…

_____
_____
_____
_____
_____
_____

January 12

Grow in the Word

As newborn babes, desire the pure milk of the word, that you may grow thereby, if indeed you have tasted that the Lord is gracious.

—1 Peter 2:2–3

Many people feel that once they have accepted Christ their job is over. They live their lives as if they were meant to sit back and enjoy the ride! But we are called to "eat" God's Word and grow. We are called to action and must not be content to stay with milk; we are to move on to the meat of the Word and mature as believers (Hebrews 5:12–14, KJV).

In her Bible study *To Live Is Christ*, Beth Moore says, "No matter how God has prepared us in advance, when we surrender our lives to serve God, we are not fully grown. In fact, the greatest challenges to learn and grow are ahead!"[2]

Meet your challenges head on and watch what happens in your life as God continues to grow you in His Word.

Prayer

Dear Lord, sometimes I am afraid to grow because I don't know what it will require. Please help me remember that You will always give me the means to carry out what I have been called to do, no matter how difficult it may seem…

_____
_____
_____
_____
_____
_____

January 13

Search the Scriptures

These were more fair-minded than those in Thessalonica, in that they received the word with all readiness, and searched the Scriptures daily to find out whether these things were so.

—Acts 17:11

Listening to your pastor or Sunday school teacher each week and not touching your Bible the rest of the week is like being spoon-fed the Word. Many believers are content to do just that—let someone else feed them, without ever checking their words against the Bible for accuracy. Beth Moore included this story in her Bible study *To Live Is Christ:*

> Some years ago, a national forest had to close off a portion of the park to tourists. A number of bears starved to death during the time the park was closed. They had grown so accustomed to being fed by the tourists, they had ceased feeding themselves.[3]

If your spiritual park were to close, would you starve to death? Do not depend on others to feed you. Pick up the Bible and feed yourself! God wants you to grow spiritually as well as physically.

Prayer

Heavenly Father, remind me to always check the accuracy of what others tell me against Your Word. Please help me to learn to feed myself spiritually and not depend on someone else to do it for me...

January 14

Blessed Beyond Measure

"Bring all the tithes into the storehouse, That there may be food in My house, And try Me now in this," says the Lord of hosts, "If I will not open for you the windows of heaven And pour out for you such blessing That there will not be room enough to receive it."

—Malachi 3:10

Church attendance and tithing are not requirements for salvation. Over the years, many have used this as an excuse for not attending church or giving financially to the Lord. Although one's salvation does not depend on church attendance or giving, God does desire that believers attend a place of worship. And He is the one who asks us to bring our tithes into the storehouse (our church) on a regular basis. He uses us to meet the monetary needs of the Body of Christ: church maintenance, discipleship training, benevolence, missions, and outreach ministries. It would be easy for God to meet these needs all on His own. But by using us, God can bestow blessings on Christians that we cannot conceive as we seek to obey His commands and carry out His ordinances.

Prayer

Lord, please help me to be faithful in church attendance and in tithing. I am not seeking to please others—only You. It is through my obedience that I am truly blessed…

January 15

One Nation Under God

Blessed is the nation whose God is the Lord, The people He has chosen as His own inheritance.

—Psalm 33:12

America is losing her blessing. Once a nation under God, we have taken God out of almost everything. We cannot pray or read the Bible in our public schools; the Ten Commandments cannot be displayed on walls of public buildings; soon we may not be able to say under God in the Pledge of Allegiance; abortions are legal and gay marriages condoned. We are no longer a nation whose god is the Lord God; we have found new gods.

Change can begin one step at a time with you and me. Take a moment to ask yourself who or what the god of your life is. Have you placed God on a shelf at the back of your closet? Who rules your home and your children? As you reflect on this Scripture, prepare in your heart to make the changes in your life that will be a first step toward helping America return to being "one nation under God."

Prayer

Lord, please remind me to do what I can in my life to make an impact for You in my country. Help me to remember to pray for the leaders of America who make decisions daily that affect each of us…

January 16

When Satan Knocks

You are of God, little children, and have overcome them, because He who is in you is greater than he who is in the world.

—1 John 4:4

Our children today are growing up in a tough, unemotional world. They are calloused to the reality and harshness of violent death, which is portrayed on television, in movies, and in video games as being "normal." Satan is behind all of this evil and is ecstatic when he wins the soul of another child.

We, as believers, need to remember that God is greater than Satan; no matter how circumstances may appear, God is in control. Our children need to be taught that God is the answer to everything and has already overcome Satan. We must teach them to let God answer the door when Satan knocks. They need to know that the battle belongs to the Lord.

Prayer

Father, I know You are greater than Satan. Help me to remember that he has no control over me unless I give it to him. Help me to teach my children about Your awesome power…

January 17

In Control

For if a man does not know how to rule his own house, how will he take care of the church of God?

—1 Timothy 3:5

Man was given the responsibility by God to be the head of the home. This does not mean that he is to be a dictator or that his wife is insignificant but that he is to be in control of his house as the final authority, answerable to God. Being in control includes being a good steward, a disciplinarian, a teacher of God's Word to his children, and most important of all, a good example. Wives and children need to see a godly man in action—not hear what one should be. When a man can control his own home and children, God can then use him in caring for the Church.

If you are married, lift the head of your home in prayer. Pray that your husband will be a man who stands firm on the Word and will be worthy of the call to serve in your church in a greater capacity.

Prayer

Father, please help me to be a good steward of the family You have given me by reminding me to pray for them. Thank You for the privilege of being able to pray for my husband. Please help him to be the man of God You have called him to be…

January 18

Change Begins with Us

"If My people who are called by My name will humble themselves, and pray and seek My face, and turn from their wicked ways, then I will hear from heaven, and will forgive their sin and heal their land."

—2 Chronicles 7:14

Change in our nation begins with God's people; healing in our nation begins with God's people. He asks us to humble ourselves, to pray, and to earnestly seek Him. Healing comes through confessing our sins, repenting, and changing our ways. It is important for us to get known sin out of our lives so that our prayers are not hindered.

Are you content with your world as it is, or are you ready for change? I am ready for change. Let's change together. I believe it is time for God's people to unite and hit the floor on bent knee so that He can heal our land.

Prayer

Cleanse my heart, oh God, so that I can pray for my nation. Please touch the hearts of Your people and unite us in prayer. Let the change begin today…

January 19

A Separate People

For they loved the praise of men more than the praise of God.

—John 12:43

Being politically correct is the accepted thing today. Everyone wants to be approved of and liked. All lifestyles are to be tolerated, and no one wants to be the one who points a finger. But God calls His people to be separate. We are not to fall in with or be deceived by how the world views sin.

Do you desire the praise of men more than the praise of God? It takes courage to buck the crowd and take a stand for what is right. Forget about being politically correct and the most popular kid on the block; take a stand for God today. Live by the standards found in His Word and seek the praise of your heavenly Father.

Prayer

Once again, Precious Lord, I find myself falling short. Please give me the courage to stand alone if need be—courage to stand on Your Word…

January 20

God Cares

Be anxious for nothing, but in everything by prayer and supplication, with thanksgiving, let your requests be made known to God; and the peace of God, which surpasses all understanding, will guard your hearts and minds through Christ Jesus.

—Philippians 4:6–7

During trials and tribulations, do you have peace? If you are a believer, you should have. God says we are to be anxious about nothing. We are to bring everything to God. We are to bring our nation and leaders before God, letting Him know that we care about our country. We are to bring our children before God and raise them in the Word so that they might gain wisdom. We are to bring all of our needs to God, trusting that He will provide. As we bring everything before our heavenly Father and then trust in Him, a peace that surpasses all of the world's understanding is given to us. What a testimony to an unsaved world!

Paul told Timothy to continue in the things he had learned as a child—to learn the Scriptures "which are able to make you wise for salvation through faith which is in Christ Jesus" (2 Timothy 3:15). When we teach our children to turn to God to meet all their needs, they are raised with a peace that their world desperately needs.

Prayer

There is nothing too small for You, Lord. Please remind me to come to You with all of the trials of life, praising and thanking You for being faithful...

_____

_____

_____

_____

_____

January 21

Continuous Praise

I will bless the Lord at all times; His praise shall continually be in my mouth.

—Psalm 34:1

Praising the Lord should be spontaneous and continuous. It should be a part of our lives whether we are on top of the mountain or in the deepest valley.

King David probably found it hard to praise God when his son died (2 Samuel 12:16–23); I found it hard to praise God as my eighteen-month-old granddaughter was being airlifted to the hospital with head trauma from a fall. But just as God was with David during his mourning, so was God with my family and me as we prayed. I praised God for little Zoë's life, for being in control of the situation, for the power He had to heal her instantly if He chose to, and for knowing if it was the right time to take her home to be with Him.

God chose to heal our baby girl, but I am so thankful that I found the strength through Him to praise Him when I did not know what the outcome would be. Is your relationship with God close enough to enable you to praise Him in all things?

Prayer

Father, please help me to grow in my relationship with You so that I will be able to give thanks in all things…

January 22

A Balanced Body

For in fact the body is not one member but many...But now God has set the members, each one of them, in the body just as He pleased.

—1 Corinthians 12:14,18

The Church is the Body of Christ. Each member has a job to do to make the Body operate effectively; each member is important to the whole. Even the "little toes" in a church are important. In our physical body, the little toe provides balance; balance is also necessary in the Church. If each member—whether a head, arm, leg or little toe—does what God calls him or her to do, the Body will be in balance.

Is your church out of balance because you are not doing what God has placed you there to do? He put you in your church for a reason. If you do not already know what that reason is, ask Him to reveal it to you today. Then begin to do what He has called you to do so that your church may become a balanced body.

Prayer

Father, whether I am to be a head, a hand, a foot or just a little toe, please help me to be the best I can be for You. Give me a willing heart to obey when I hear Your call...

January 23

Family Encouragement

But exhort one another daily, while it is called "Today," lest any of you be hardened through the deceitfulness of sin.

—Hebrews 3:13

It is easy to become discouraged in our walk with the Lord. Everything around us exudes the pleasures of life and affords temptations and distractions. God knew that we would need encouragement, so He gave us our church families. Not only are we to worship together, we are also to deeply care for one another. Pray for the hurting sister; lend a hand to help our brother; provide for the physical needs of the one experiencing hard times; and most important of all, love one another and hold each other accountable.

It is much harder to be led astray or tempted when you are surrounded by the love of a godly family. Allow your church family to minister to you, and in turn, you will be ready to minister to others.

Prayer

Thank You, Lord, for my church family. Let me love them the way You love me. Help me to be open to all encouragement and accept any discipline in love…

January 24

Be a Mountain Mover

In those days there was no king in Israel; everyone did what was right in his own eyes.

—Judges 17:6

America seems to be following in Old Testament Israel's footsteps. Many of today's leaders have not chosen to follow God's law. For example, a recent president's morals were questionable, yet society was willing to let bygones be bygones. This man was not held accountable to God's moral law and made to pay a price, because society itself loves doing what feels good more than it loves justice; society loves doing what it wants to do.

As God's people, it is our responsibility to be in daily prayer for our leaders and our country; we can make a change. Remember, the faithful prayers of one believer can move mountains (Matthew 17:20). Are you a mountain mover?

Prayer

Give Your Church a heart for prayer, Lord. Please forgive us for not bringing our leaders before You daily. Remind us that You can and do move mountains on our behalf…

January 25

Help from Above

Fear not, for I am with you; Be not dismayed, for I am your God. I will strengthen you, Yes, I will help you, I will uphold you with My righteous right hand.

—Isaiah 41:10

The terrors of life surround us. We see it every day in the papers and on television and hear it on the radio: wars, floods, famines, droughts, tornadoes, hurricanes, and murders in our schools—the list is endless. But as children of God, we need not fear. He can give us a peace that the people of this world cannot understand.

When others are afraid and hurting, the Church can minister to them more effectively than when they are healthy and prosperous. Hurting people will run to a physician quicker than healthy people will. Be on the lookout for a hurting and fearful person today and share the source of your strength with them. It may be your witness and testimony that will help lead that person to the Great Physician—our help from above.

Prayer

Father, please remind me not to be fearful when terrors surround me. You will strengthen and guide me with Your awesome power and right hand…

January 26

Glory and Honor

Give unto the Lord the glory due to His name; Worship the Lord in the beauty of holiness.

—Psalm 29:2

God deserves our glory and praise. What better place could there be to give God glory than in church with His people?

As an active participant on my church's worship team, I cannot tell you how blessed I am by watching my sisters and brothers in Christ praising the Lord together in song. When hundreds of people lift their voices in praise to God, things happen! The Spirit begins to move, people are touched, and lives are changed.

Did you give God the glory, honor, and praise due Him in your place of worship this week? If not, plan to be in church next Sunday. Begin your new week by praising the Lord with other believers.

Prayer

Father, I love to praise You. Thank You for providing me with a church home where I am free to worship openly. I give all glory and honor to You…

January 27

Through God's Eyes

But the Lord said to Samuel, "Do not look at his appearance or at his physical stature, because I have refused him. For the Lord does not see as man sees; for man looks at the outward appearance, but the Lord looks at the heart."

—1 Samuel 16:7

Samuel was to anoint God's chosen man to rule after Saul. As all of Jesse's sons passed by Samuel, God reminded him not to look on the outward appearance but to the inner man—the heart. David, Jesse's youngest son, would have seemed the least likely to become king, given his age and appearance. But David had a heart for the things of the Lord. He would be the successor to the throne, and God used this "little boy," David, in mighty ways.

Do you have a heart for the things of the Lord? God is not looking at your appearance; ask Him to change your heart today. He can use you in ways beyond anything you can imagine; He can use you to slay giants.

Prayer

Lord, as the chorus I sing in church says, change my heart and make it in the likeness of You…

January 28

Clothed in Righteousness

The eyes of the Lord are in every place, Keeping watch on the evil and the good.

—Proverbs 15:3

Men cannot run from God. He is omnipresent—everywhere. There is nothing done in this world that He does not see. Why, then, do we spend so much time running from God? Because if we stop and face Him, we will have to stop doing the things of this world—the things that call out to our sin nature. Once you become a child of God, you must put away evil things. God will clothe you in righteousness, and your desire will be to do those things that are true, honest, and good (Philippians 4:8).

Are you tired of running from God? Submit to Him today. It is far less tiring to submit to His ways than to continually run from Him.

Prayer

I long to have a life clothed with Your righteousness, Lord. Please forgive me and cleanse my heart today...

January 29

The Winning Team

Be sober, be vigilant; because your adversary the devil walks about like a roaring lion, seeking whom he may devour.

—1 Peter 5:8

Satan wants you! He is constantly roaming the earth looking for victims. But God wants you more than Satan does. He loves you so much that while you were still a sinner, He sent His only Son to die on the cross so that you could become His child (Romans 5:8). What did Satan do for you? Absolutely nothing! He is selfish, cold, cruel, destructive, and according to 1 John 4:4, a loser.

Do you want to be on the losing team or the winning team? God is waiting for you to seek Him. He will send the Comforter to you; all you have to do is ask Jesus into your life. Do not become Satan's victim. Let God fight the battle for you when Satan comes roaring at your door.

Prayer

Thank You for the gifts of grace, forgiveness, and mercy, Lord. I do not want to become Satan's victim. Please become Lord of my life today; I want to be part of Your winning team…

January 30

Laborers with God

For we are God's fellow workers; you are God's field, you are God's building.
—1 Corinthians 3:9

God desires us to labor with Him, not only for Him. He has a plan and wants us to be part of it (Jeremiah 29:11). In *Experiencing God* Henry Blackaby tells us that God is already working here on earth. We need only to look around us to see where He is working and join Him, using our spiritual gifts.[4] If you are not already serving in a local church, ask God to lead you to one that is biblically sound. Watch to see where God is working—then join Him in His work. As you begin to use your spiritual gifts, you will begin to produce godly fruit and the Church will grow.

Prayer

Father, I know You are at work in this world. I want to be part of heaven here on earth. Please help me to continually seek to do Your will…

January 31

Uncharted Waters

But as it is written: "Eye has not seen, nor ear heard, Nor have entered into the heart of man The things which God has prepared for those who love Him."

—1 Corinthians 2:9

Because we are children of God, there are things waiting for us that are beyond our natural capabilities. Our basic human nature is to be afraid of the unknown; there is safety in the familiar. But God often leads us into uncharted waters. Although we may be afraid of the task before us, God is our refuge and strength (Psalm 46:1); when we feel like we are sinking, God will extend His hand for us to hold on to, just as He did to Peter (Matthew 14:31). If our focus is on God, He will keep us above the water.

God will help you accomplish more than you could attempt to do on your own. This book of devotions is beyond anything I could have imagined doing for God; I could not have done it on my own. As He has helped me, so too will He help you.

God made you; He loves you. He can lead you through the uncharted waters of your life. Allow Him to be your navigator, and you will have the cruise of your life!

Prayer

Father, You are the great I Am (Exodus 3:14). I want You to chart every day of my life. Please remind me that I can do great and mighty things when You are in control…

February

February 1

A Closer Walk

Oh come, let us worship and bow down; let us kneel before the Lord our Maker.

—Psalm 95:6

Every day lived in the Lord is beautiful. Especially beautiful is the day we come together to worship as a corporate body in song and praise. God created us to worship Him—to have fellowship with Him. Bowing before the Lord shows our reverence for God and our submission to His authority in our lives.

Do you have a right relationship with your Maker? As you worship this week, ask God to draw you closer to Him; He is able and faithful to do this when you sincerely desire a closer walk and seek Him with your whole heart.

Prayer

I love You, Lord. You are the light of my life. I worship and adore You…

February 2

Garden Prayer

I desire therefore that the men pray everywhere, lifting up holy hands, without wrath and doubting.

—1 Timothy 2:8

One of the most memorable phrases I have ever seen on a wall hanging reads, "One is nearer to God's heart in a garden than anywhere else on earth." Because I am a gardener at heart, that plaque is hanging on my kitchen wall. What better place could there be to lift up holy hands to the Lord and come before Him, just as you are, than in a garden? God communed with Adam and Eve in the perfect garden, the Garden of Eden. "Pray everywhere" gives us the freedom to lift our hands and pray regardless of our surroundings. All that is needed for quality time in prayer is a pure heart, which can be taken with you to your garden anytime—just you, lifting your hands to God in prayer and praise.

Have you walked with God in a garden lately?

Prayer

Lord, I am thankful that You reside in the garden of my heart. Please remind me that wherever You are is holy ground, even if it is only in my backyard...

February 3

A Solitary Place

Now in the morning, having risen a long while before daylight, He went out and departed to a solitary place; and there He prayed.

—Mark 1:35

Why do Christians need to pray? Because Jesus, our example, prayed. He created this world, performed miracles, and raised the dead, yet He prayed daily. He went off by Himself to a lonely place while it was still morning to seek His Father's will and put His day into the Father's hands. If Jesus felt the need to begin each day with prayer, doesn't it make sense that we as human beings need to develop this habit?

The Lord has been convicting me of the shortcomings in my prayer life. Is He convicting you? If so, submit to Jesus and then ask Him to meet you on your knees as you seek Him early in the morning in your solitary place.

Prayer

Father, I do not come to You in prayer as often as I should. I fail to pray for others, because I allow life to get in the way. Prayer is my direct phone line to You; remind me to use it every day…

February 4

Delighted Through You

Delight yourself also in the Lord, And He shall give you the desires of your heart.

—Psalm 37:4

Even as Christians, many of us have the "give-me syndrome": give me this; give me that. God does not have a problem with giving us things. He does have a problem with our always asking and never giving back in return. He does have a problem with our not seeking His will. God places the condition of "delighting yourself in the Lord" when promising to give us the desires of our heart.

Are you continually asking God to do something in your life, but not spending time developing a relationship with Him? Is God asking something of you that you are not willing to give? Ask the Lord to show you what you can do today to bring Him delight.

Prayer

Father, sometimes I forget my part in our relationship. Help me to remember that You desire me to worship and obey—that You desire me to delight myself in You…

February 5

Seek the Lord

The Lord is good to those who wait for Him, To the soul who seeks Him.
—Lamentations 3:25

When something is lost, a great deal of energy and effort go into finding it. The Lord tells us in our spiritual life to "seek, and you will find"(Matthew 7:7). Seeking requires time, effort, and a sincere desire to find what you are looking for; seeking the Lord requires Bible reading, prayer, fellowship, service, and giving. Many are not ready to put that much effort into finding the Lord and seeking His will. How sad that they are missing out on the best things in life!

Spend time today before the Lord, waiting on Him. Fellowship with God is sweet when you seek Him with all of your heart.

Prayer

Lord, I desire a relationship with You, which requires time and effort. Please be patient with me as I learn to seek You wholeheartedly…

February 6

Great and Mighty Things

"Call to Me, and I will answer you, and show you great and mighty things, which you do not know."

—Jeremiah 33:3

God has wonderful things planned for His children. Unfortunately, most of us want to operate with only what we can see. It is difficult for us to take the step of faith that allows us to participate in the "great and mighty things" that God has purposed in His heart for us to do.

Think of all the discoveries made because people believed in themselves; how much more could be accomplished if our belief was in God? If we allow Him to, God will give us a life beyond anything we can imagine. Our lives will change and God's Kingdom will be advanced if we are simply willing.

Are you willing to step out in faith and accept the unknown that God has planned for you?

Prayer

Lord, please give me the faith I need to call upon Your name. I want to participate in the wonderful things You have planned for me…

February 7

Into His Light

But you are a chosen generation, a royal priesthood, a holy nation, His own special people, that you may proclaim the praises of Him who called you out of darkness into His marvelous light.

—1 Peter 2:9

With salvation comes responsibility. We are to go forth into our neighborhoods and workplaces and share Jesus Christ. He is the light of the world and desires that all should come out of darkness into the light.

Is your light shining bright enough that your neighbors and coworkers know you serve Christ? Do they see something in you that makes you stand out from others? Share the light of your life today with someone in darkness—they may be tired of stumbling.

Prayer

Jesus, You are the light of my life. Thank You for choosing me and setting me apart. Give me the boldness I need to share my light with someone who is alone in the dark…

February 8

Glory to God

Now to Him who is able to do exceedingly abundantly above all that we ask or think, according to the power that works in us, to Him be glory in the church by Christ Jesus to all generations, forever and ever. Amen.

—Ephesians 3:20–21

Jesus loves the Church; we are His bride. He wants a relationship with us that is more intimate than any other. Jesus longs to do things for us and through us. When we come together as a corporate body to worship and praise Him, we glorify His name and He rejoices.

As you sing praises and give honor and glory to the Lord in your place of worship this week, thank Him for choosing you; then eagerly wait for His return to claim you, His bride.

Prayer

Help me to be a faithful bride until Your return, Lord. As a wife longs to please her husband here on earth, I long to please and glorify You in all I do…

February 9

To Each His Own

But let each one examine his own work, and then he will have rejoicing in himself alone, and not in another.

—Galatians 6:4

There is satisfaction in a job well done. But for Christians to receive that satisfaction, hard work and commitment are required by God. We are called to do the best we can in whatever He gives us to do.

Sometimes God asks us to pray for people we do not like. That is hard for us in our sin nature and requires commitment—commitment to allow Jesus to show us through His eyes how to love the unlovable. Others may not understand why we try to love everyone. God tells us to. "This is My commandment, that you love one another as I have loved you" (John 15:12).

We are each responsible for our own behavior in God's eyes; we are each responsible to examine ourselves. As we do what God calls us to do to the best of our ability, without worrying what others think, we can have satisfaction; we can rejoice in a job well done.

Prayer

Lord, You have given me a job to do. Help me to perform it to the best of my ability. I want to rejoice in a job done well…

February 10

Yes or No

But above all, my brethren, do not swear, either by heaven or by earth or with any other oath. But let your "Yes" be "Yes," and your "No," "No," lest you fall into judgment.

—James 5:12

What a foreign concept in today's society: simply saying yes or no and meaning it. How many times has someone promised to do something for you and you heard, "I swear I will"? God wants a simple yes or no, with no swearing involved.

We learn these two short words at a very early age, yet as we grow older they seem to become harder to say. Many of us want to make excuses and skirt around an issue. God wants us to become as little children and keep our answers simple.

The next time someone asks you to do something for them, think about what you want to do; then say yes or no.

Prayer

Lord, we tend to make life more complicated than You intended it to be. Help us to remember that a simple answer is okay...

February 11

Be Not Dismayed

And he said, "Listen, all you of Judah and you inhabitants of Jerusalem, and you, King Jehoshaphat! Thus says the Lord to you: 'Do not be afraid nor dismayed because of this great multitude, for the battle is not yours, but God's.'"

—2 Chronicles 20:15

How many times do we try to fight our battles alone? We tend to forget that we are in the Lord's army, with the best Commander in the world. He does not want us to be afraid or dismayed; He wants to fight the battle for us.

There may be a private war going on in your life right now. It may be sickness, depression, fear of failed relationships, decisions to make that affect others, or financial problems. Whatever you are battling, remember that you are not alone. God wants to win the war for you if you will allow Him to take command. Turn your battle over to Him.

Prayer

Take my life, Lord. Make me wholly Yours. I want You to fight my battles for me, because You are always victorious…

February 12

Our Refuge and Strength

Trust in Him at all times, you people; Pour out your heart before Him; God is a refuge for us. Selah.

—Psalm 62:8

It is easy to trust in God when you are on top of the world. But when disaster strikes, do you still trust Him? God has promised that "all things work together for good to those who love God" (Romans 8:28). When hard times come, God wants us to seek Him, to cry out to Him, and to continue to trust Him.

We are God's children, and He wants the best for us. Sometimes what we think is best is not His best. We cannot always understand why God allows certain situations into our lives. We do not need to understand; we only need to trust in the God who created us. He will finish the work that He began.

Prayer

Lord, I do not always understand the situations in my life, but I trust You. Please be my Refuge and Strength, especially when I am weary and feel alone…

February 13

It Is Hard...

But as for you, brethren, do not grow weary in doing good.

—2 Thessalonians 3:13

It is hard to continue being nice to someone when they reciprocate with rudeness or insolence. It is hard to always be the one to make coffee each week before Sunday morning services. It is hard to always be the first one to say hello. It is hard to smile at a neighbor who has belittled you. It is hard to help the handicapped woman you meet at the grocery store each week. It is hard to get up in the middle of the night to take a friend to the hospital. It is hard to pray for someone when you feel overwhelmed or exhausted. It was hard for Jesus to be crucified on the cross for you and me—but He did it.

Continue in your good works, my friend. Jesus did what was hard so that you and I, through His strength, can do what is hard. It is easier to do the things we are tired of doing when we remember we are doing them for Jesus.

Prayer

When I feel weary of always doing the right thing, please give me Your strength, Lord. Remind me that although the gift of salvation on the cross was hard for You, Your love for me was greater than the pain You endured...

February 14

On Bended Knee

Therefore God also has highly exalted Him and given Him the name which is above every name, that at the name of Jesus every knee should bow, of those in heaven, and of those on earth, and of those under the earth.

—Philippians 2:9–10

The Bible tells us that one day every knee will bow at the Name of Jesus. But in this life, God has given us freedom of choice: to bow or not to bow. It is completely up to us to make the decision to allow God to become Lord of our life; on this earth He will not force our knees to bend in worship.

We live in a country where we have the freedom to worship. Are you exercising that freedom? Have you attended a place of worship lately? Ask God to bring a body of believers into your life who can become your church family. Worship with them and freely bow down before the Name of Jesus as you give glory to God.

Prayer

I love You, Lord, and confess You before men. Help me to remember to use my freedom to worship on bended knee before that freedom is taken away…

February 15

Pleasing God

But Peter and the other apostles answered and said: "We ought to obey God rather than men."

—Acts 5:29

Success is often measured by how much money people make, the cars they drive, the clothes they wear, the clubs they belong to, or even the church they attend. How many of these "successful" people are truly happy or at peace?

I believe that the fast pace we live at today is the result of people trying to run from God. Running to God would require obedience. Most people want to avoid having to obey God, but the only true measure of success is obedience to Him. The praises showered on us by men are temporal. "Well done, good and faithful servant" is for eternity (Matthew 25:21).

In her book *To Live Is Christ*, Beth Moore says, "Hopefully, we will come to understand that, in our Christian lives, success is obedience to God, not results we can measure."[5] Often we do not see the results of our obedience, but we will experience the blessings. God sees everything we do in obedience to Him.

Prayer

Heavenly Father, as I go through my day, help me to please You in all I do. It doesn't matter what others think; You are the one I need to obey in order to find true success…

February 16

Hold on to the Promises

What then shall we say to these things? If God is for us, who can be against us?

—Romans 8:31

Life deals us garbage now and then because we live in a sinful world and, as Christians, we will not always be liked. Jesus was a good and perfect man, yet he was persecuted. As He was persecuted, so will we be. But in the midst of this world's trials and tribulations, believers have God to grab on to. He has promised in His Word that when the storms of life threaten to overtake us, if we trust in Him we will be victorious.

Take today's Scripture and hold on to it for dear life! With God on your side you can handle all the garbage that Satan can throw at you. God will be with you through the storms.

Prayer

Thank You for the promises given to me in Your Word, Lord. When trials come, I can hold on to You and know that is all I need…

February 17

God's Comfort

Blessed be the God and Father of our Lord Jesus Christ, the Father of mercies and God of all comfort, who comforts us in all our tribulation, that we may be able to comfort those who are in any trouble, with the comfort with which we ourselves are comforted by God.

—2 Corinthians 1:3–4

I believe that God allows every believer to go through certain struggles in life to help us minister more effectively to those in need. Who better can comfort a victim of abortion than one who has felt the pain of having an abortion yet also has experienced the healing forgiveness and love that comes from Christ? Who could be a better witness of God's sustaining strength than Joni Eareckson Tada, bound to her wheelchair yet faithfully serving God? A person who has lost a spouse or a child can better comfort someone dealing with death than the best counselor who has never faced a personal loss.

God uses all of your experiences to enable you to comfort others dealing with the realities of living in this world. As you go about your daily routine today, look for someone to comfort. God doesn't want your experiences to go to waste.

Prayer

Heavenly Father, thank You for the tribulations that You have comforted me through. May I return that comfort to others and help them find the healing that comes from You…

February 18

Called to Action

But be doers of the word, and not hearers only, deceiving yourselves.

—James 1:22

God's Word calls us to act upon what we read or hear in the Scriptures. It is difficult to be "doers" if we do not know what we are supposed to be doing. That is why we have the Bible as our "manual for life." Each believer needs to be responsible for searching the Scriptures daily for themselves. This not only helps us to recognize wrong teachings but also enables us to put into practice the words that we read.

Being a witness for Christ requires action. You cannot be a couch potato and be an effective disciple for Christ. Ask God to help you put into practice the truth He reveals to you today.

Prayer

Lord, please help me to be an active Christian. Let everything I do be a reflection of You, so that others may come to know Your love and grace…

February 19

Holy Fear

And to man He said, "Behold, the fear of the Lord, that is wisdom, And to depart from evil is understanding."

—Job 28:28

God is love. If God is love, why should we fear Him? We are not to be afraid of God but to hold a holy reverence for Him. It is wise to consider the judge. Our earthly judges are treated with respect. Should our heavenly Father, our ultimate Judge, be treated with any less respect?

I want to receive a sentence of life, not death, from my heavenly Judge. Understanding what He wants from me here on earth is very pertinent to how I live my life. My salvation is not dependent on how I live, but the way I live my life bears witness to the fact that I respect and fear my God.

Do you have a healthy fear of the Lord? Seek wisdom and understanding as you live your life reverently for Him.

Prayer

Lord, teach me Your ways. Please help me to act upon the wisdom and understanding that You reveal to me through the Word. Give me a holy fear for the ways of God…

February 20

Our Invisible Strength

Some trust in chariots, and some in horses; But we will remember the name of the Lord our God.

—Psalm 20:7

It is easy to trust in something visible when you face a battle. People in Bible days trusted in their war chariots and horses to win their battles. In modern times, our soldiers have much more sophisticated modes of transportation and weapons, yet the world is still without peace and hope.

If only everyone could truly see the God who is Creator of all! When we get to know and trust Him, every battle becomes His. We no longer need to trust the visible; the invisible becomes our source of strength.

Prayer

Lord, I am so thankful that I can call upon Your name. Even though I cannot see You, I feel Your presence in my life and see You working around me…

February 21

Hugs from Jesus

But each one is tempted when he is drawn away by his own desires and enticed.

—James 1:14

Holding one another accountable to God's Word is just one of the many functions of the Church. It is much more difficult to give in to temptations and selfish desires when we have people surrounding us who are encouragers and prayer warriors. God wants us to receive a crown of life and says that we are blessed when we can withstand the temptations and trials here on earth (James 1:12).

I know that I am thankful for my church family and appreciate the love, prayers, and encouragement showered upon me by them. They remind me to lean on God when I want to rely on myself to resist temptations.

A hug of encouragement from one of my church family members is like getting a hug from Jesus. Have you had a hug from Jesus this week?

Prayer

Lord, thank You for the people who have been placed in my life. Hugs from them are like hugs from You. I love the encouragement and the accountability they provide…

February 22

Trust Him

For we are His workmanship, created in Christ Jesus for good works, which God prepared beforehand that we should walk in them.

—Ephesians 2:10

Did you know that God had a plan for your life before you were born? He knew you and had you covered while you were still in your mother's womb (Psalm 139). How awesome to know that God is in control and has a plan, because sometimes we don't do very well on our own! We often take little side trips on life's journey, but our heavenly Father knows what our destination is and gets us back on course. Some of us are a bit more stubborn about finding and obeying His will, but the outcome is always the same—He wins. Even Satan, the master of deceit, cannot win against God.

If you have been struggling with something God is calling you to do, submit to Him today. Your journey will be much more enjoyable when you allow God to be your guide and help you avoid the pitfalls Satan likes to place in your path.

Prayer

You truly are omniscient, Lord. Help me to fully trust You as my guide on my journey. Please help me to fulfill the plan You have for my life…

_____

_____

_____

_____

_____

February 23

Redeeming the Time

Therefore He says: "Awake, you who sleep, Arise from the dead, And Christ will give you light." See then that you walk circumspectly, not as fools but as wise, redeeming the time, because the days are evil. Therefore do not be unwise, but understand what the will of the Lord is.

—Ephesians 5:14–17

How many times as a child did you hear the phrase "Waste not—want not?" Have you ever thought of that phrase in the context of sharing God's Word? I believe we are entering—if not already in—the end times. Time for us to share the gospel is getting short.

How much of your life have you wasted not accomplishing anything for God? I will be the first to admit that I have wasted a lot of my time. In the twelfth chapter of Ecclesiastes, Solomon urges us to not waste our youth but to serve the Lord while we have energy and good health. But it is also important to remember to not look back if you have used your time unwisely (Philippians 3:13). Confess your shortcomings to the Lord, and use whatever time you may have left to freely share the gospel of Jesus Christ, redeeming the time, until the Lord's return.

Prayer

Lord, please help me to be a good steward of the time You have given me here on earth. There are many who need to know the plan of salvation. Help me to freely share that gift to those You place in my path…

_____

_____

_____

_____

_____

_____

February 24

Nowhere to Run

Where can I go from Your Spirit? Or where can I flee from Your presence?
—Psalm 139:7

Hiding from God is impossible. Adam and Eve tried to hide from God after eating the forbidden fruit. When God asked them where they were, the question was just a formality; He knew where they were, and why.

Are you trying to hide from God? Dear friend, do not waste your energy. Once you are His child, there is nowhere to run and nowhere to hide. He will allow you a loose leash but will tighten it when He sees you straying too far. Run to Him with open arms and ask Him to reveal His plan for you. Exerting energy for God's cause is far less tiring than running from His presence.

Prayer

Father, You began a good work in me and will complete it. Help me to not hinder You by running away…

February 25

Focused on Christ

The Lord is my strength and my shield; My heart trusted in Him, and I am helped; Therefore my heart greatly rejoices, And with my song I will praise Him.

—Psalm 28:7

We as believers often try to do things in our own strength and fail. The Lord wants to be our Strength and Protector. In order for Him to be those things to us, we need to trust Him completely. That means we trust Him "for better or worse, for richer or poorer, in sickness and in health, 'til death us do part." Wow—what a concept! We are married to Christ and need to trust Him completely with our lives.

When we allow Christ to be our Strength, we find great joy and can praise Him even when life seems unbearable and we feel we are sinking. God will help us keep our head above the water when we are focused on Him and are relying on His strength.

Prayer

Heavenly Father, thank You for being with me until the day I die. Please give me the strength to hold on to You tightly and never let go…

February 26

A Divine Purpose

That we who first trusted in Christ should be to the praise of His glory.

—Ephesians 1:12

Every believer has a purpose: to glorify God through faith in Jesus Christ. Service to God begins with a daily walk with Christ. As we develop our personal relationship with Jesus, we long to glorify Him and Him alone.

Our gifts and talents were given to us to glorify God and to edify the body of believers. Reading God's Word and talking with Him daily strengthens our relationship and gives us the knowledge we need to glorify Him. Everything we do should be done with the desire to be Christlike.

As you spend time with God each day, ask Him what He would have you do to bring glory to His name.

Prayer

Dear Lord, please help me to take self out of my life. Help me to put You first and always try to glorify Your name…

February 27

Unto the Lord

Not with eyeservice, as men-pleasers, but as bondservants of Christ, doing the will of God from the heart, with goodwill doing service, as to the Lord, and not to men.

—Ephesians 6:6–7

Do you have a heart for the things of God? If so, your treasures should not be here on earth and pleasing men should be the last thing on your mind: "For where your treasure is, there your heart will be also" (Matthew 6:21).

God is a jealous God and does not permit us to have any other gods before Him (Exodus 20:3). He wants us to serve Him with our whole heart (Psalm 119:2). Serving Him wholly can be difficult to do when the pressures and demands of family and workplace are tossing us around and dividing our hearts. But if we will spend a few minutes with Him at the beginning of each day, everything else will fall into place. We will be in tune with God when He strums the strings of our hearts.

Prayer

I love You, Lord. It is my desire to serve You with my whole heart. Please help me keep my focus and my priorities in order…

February 28

Love in Abundance

Therefore, as we have opportunity, let us do good to all, especially to those who are of the household of faith.

—Galatians 6:10

"Charity begins at home." If everyone believed that statement, our families would not be falling apart. Charity is love, and love cares for its own. God wants us to love our families and to provide for them. If we are so busy taking care of the needs of the world that we forget those closest to us, God frowns. He does want our love to extend to our fellow believers and beyond, but if we serve in our churches seven days a week to the neglect of our families, our priorities are wrong.

First take time for your loved ones in the circle of your family; then extend that love to others. God will see to it that there is love in abundance so that you can care for all those He places in your life.

Prayer

Help me, Father, to remember to care for the people You have placed in my immediate family first. May I extend to them the same love and kindness You show me…

February 29

My Refuge and Strength

God is our refuge and strength, A very present help in trouble.

—Psalm 46:1

It takes courage to be strong in the Lord. It requires us to give up the "I can do it better than anyone else" mentality. We are such control freaks that, for some of us, giving complete control to God is often impossible. During trials and tribulations, we may make an effort to allow God to be our strength, but we grab back the control when fear begins to take over. God loves us and wants us to run to Him for shelter when storms arise. He wants to tuck us under His wings and protect us from the wind and rain the way a mother hen protects her chicks (Luke 13:34).

Ask God to become your strength and hiding place. Allow Him to have complete control over your troubles, and, despite the raging storms, you will have peace.

Prayer

Lord, please be the strength of my heart, my very present help when the troubles of life overwhelm me. I want to feel the peace that refuge in You brings to my life...

March

March 1

Be Strong in the Lord

Then you will prosper, if you take care to fulfill the statutes and judgments with which the Lord charged Moses concerning Israel. Be strong and of good courage; do not fear nor be dismayed.

—1 Chronicles 22:13

Although King David made the initial preparations for the construction of God's temple, he would not be allowed to build it. God reminded David of the many wars he had fought and the blood he had shed; therefore, David was not worthy to build the temple. Instead, God chose David's son, Solomon, a man of peace (1 Chronicles 22:7–10). Solomon was given a very difficult task, but David reminded him to be strong and have faith. David knew that God would be with Solomon and would provide him with the strength and courage he needed to complete his God-ordained task.

Every believer has a God-ordained task. Do you know what yours is? If not, ask Him to show you what He wants you to do. Then take strength and courage from God and face your task with shoulders squared and head held high.

Prayer

Lord, sometimes the things You give me to do seem impossible to complete. Thank You for being the source of my energy and giving me the strength to do Your will…

March 2

Before the Sun Goes Down

"Be angry, and do not sin": do not let the sun go down on your wrath, nor give place to the devil.

—Ephesians 4:26–27

Most people who are angry want the whole world to know it. Furthermore, they want to feel angry until they are ready to resolve the problem—even if it takes days, months, or years. God has a different agenda for His children. Although there is a righteous anger, in God's Word we are urged to settle our disputes at the end of each day, to the best of our ability. In His wisdom God knew that the longer a wound festers, the harder it is to heal.

Forgiving and putting away anger is often difficult for even the most devoted believer. But when we depend on God and His strength, we can obey the Word. Peaceful sleep comes to those who have settled each day's problems before a new day begins.

Prayer

Heavenly Father, please help me to allow You to soften my heart when I do not feel like putting away my anger. Remind me to settle disputes before the sun goes down each day…

March 3

Baby Steps

The Lord is my light and my salvation; Whom shall I fear? The Lord is the strength of my life; Of whom shall I be afraid?

—Psalm 27:1

A baby's first step is an exciting moment; it can also be very scary for the baby. But Mom or Dad are usually there to cheer, encourage, and pick the baby up when he or she tumbles.

God is a believer's heavenly Parent. The first steps in our Christian walk can be very frightening and we may tumble, but God is always there to pick us up. New challenges and horizons wait for us as we take those first steps and gain strength and confidence to wander farther. With each step we become stronger, confident that our heavenly Father is there to pick us up when we fall. We don't need to be afraid as we continue our walk in the Lord.

Dear friend, new and exciting things are waiting for you. Take that first baby step and experience a whole new world. God will be there to cheer you on with each new step.

Prayer

Lord, I want to expand my world through You. Keep me safe as I stumble and learn to walk as Your child. Strengthen me with Your encouraging words…

March 4

A Song in My Heart

"Behold, God is my salvation, I will trust and not be afraid; 'for Yah, the Lord, is my strength and song; He also has become my salvation.'"

—Isaiah 12:2

I thank the Lord for not only being my salvation and my strength, but for the song He puts in my heart. Is there a song in your heart?

God desires for each of His children to have joy and to be able to sing praises to His name. There are many times when we feel we cannot sing to the Lord. We have trials and tribulations, and our hearts feel too burdened to sing. That is when we need to draw on the strength of our heavenly Father. James tells us to "count it all joy" when we face temptations and trials (James 1:2). How does one feel joy in sorrow? By placing everything in the hand of the Lord Jehovah—He is your joy and your song.

Prayer

Heavenly Father, thank You for putting a song in my heart even when I don't feel like singing. You never fail to pick me up when I remember to call on Your name and sing Your praises…

March 5

You Are Important to God

My help comes from the Lord, Who made heaven and earth.

—Psalm 121:2

How small and insignificant I sometimes feel! God created everything in the universe, yet man is the focus of His love and mercy. No matter how small or unimportant we may see ourselves, God loved us enough to send His only Son to die a horrible death so that we could become children of God. How awesome! He desires to help us become all He intended us to be. When we draw from God's strength and allow Him to help us, there is nothing we cannot do (Philippians 4:13). We can move mountains (Matthew 17:20)!

Is there a mountain in your life? God is there to help you move it if you go to Him and let your requests be known. At that moment, you are the most important thing in the universe to Him!

Prayer

You are my help in time of need, Lord. Thank You for loving me and carrying me on Your shoulders when I am too weak to walk. Thank You for moving mountains on my behalf…

March 6

Alive in Christ

You also, as living stones, are being built up a spiritual house, a holy priesthood, to offer up spiritual sacrifices acceptable to God through Jesus Christ.

—1 Peter 2:5

The Church is to be alive. How many churches are dead today, and why are they dead? Maybe the people attending those churches are spiritually dead because they do not have a living personal relationship with Jesus Christ. Perhaps their shepherds are not teaching them truth. There may be many reasons; but whatever the reason, God is not happy with dead churches.

Are you worshipping in a church with "living stones," or is your church lifeless? As you seek to serve the Lord with all your heart, check the pulse of your church. If you cannot find a heartbeat, it may be time to ask the Lord to lead you to a new place of worship.

Prayer

Thank You, Lord, for my church of living stones. I can feel Your presence and see Your handiwork whenever I enter my place of worship. What a blessing I have in my church family…

March 7

My Yoke Is Easy

Come to Me, all you who labor and are heavy laden, and I will give you rest.
—Matthew 11:28

Nothing can compare to the rest that is found in salvation through Jesus Christ. Once we have accepted Jesus into our heart, we have a constant companion who will never leave us and will help us carry our daily burdens. Many times believers become exhausted in their daily walk and service to God because they are not drawing on God's promise that "My yoke is easy and My burden is light" (Matthew 11:30).

A yoke allows two animals to pull a load with equal weight, so that one animal is not struggling harder than the other. Yoke yourself with Christ, and He will share the weight of your burden. Every task that we endeavor to complete is made easier by the companionship and strength of our Lord and Savior, Jesus Christ.

Prayer

Father, I try too many times to carry my burdens alone. Please help me to find rest and strength in You as I tackle the tasks before me today…

March 8

Hope in the Fast Lane

Therefore my heart is glad, and my glory rejoices; My flesh also will rest in hope.

—Psalm 16:9

One of the greatest blessings for believers is the hope that comes through our faith in Jesus. No matter how tough life gets or how many obstacles Satan throws our way, we have eternal life through Jesus Christ our Lord! That fact alone should put a smile on the face of a believer, regardless of the trials of life. In our humanness, it is hard to smile when we are being run over by a truck. But when we look to God, He gives us the assurance that He will never leave us or forsake us (Deuteronomy 31:6); He will be right there under the truck with us!

Prayer

Lord, You are always with me, no matter what trials come my way. Thank You for Your faithfulness, even when I feel I am in the fast lane and about to be run over by a truck. Thank You for the hope and rest I find in You alone…

March 9

Rest in the Lord

I will both lie down in peace, and sleep; For You alone, O Lord, make me dwell in safety.

—Psalm 4:8

Guns, bars on home windows, guard dogs, car and house alarms, pepper spray—who can feel safe in today's world? A believer can! Once a person becomes a Christian, they can have peace and security. Sure, we still need to take precautions and use wisdom in our daily lives, but we can rest in God's promise that He will keep us safe.

Does that mean that physical harm will never come to believers and their families? No. But it does mean that we have the security of knowing that even in the worst-case scenario, we have safety in the knowledge that we will be with God for eternity—that is our security blanket.

Prayer

Thank You, Father, for the peace and rest that come through knowing You. I am secure in the knowledge of Your love and infinite wisdom…

The Old Paths

Thus says the Lord: "Stand in the ways and see, And ask for the old paths, where the good way is, And walk in it; Then you will find rest for your souls. But they said, 'We will not walk in it.'"

—Jeremiah 6:16

Jeremiah warned the tribe of Benjamin about their stubbornness toward God. They would be judged for leaving "the old paths."

Christians today are no different than those ancestors of Benjamin. We think we know better than God does the paths we should take. We leave the Lord's path and run into all kinds of unseen obstacles, yet He is right there with us. He watches on the sidelines and waits for us to ask Him to lead us back to the old path, the well-worn path that leads to peace and eternal life through Jesus Christ our Lord.

Do not be stubborn like the children of Benjamin; enjoy your peace and rest as you walk the old paths marked out for you in God's Word.

Prayer

Father, please protect me from my own stubborn ways. Help me to walk in Your paths and not in paths of my own making…

March 11

Practice Makes Perfect

Rest in the Lord, and wait patiently for Him.

—Psalm 37:7

Rest seems to be only a word, not something one does, and patience is not a virtue for most people. God asks us to do both: rest and wait patiently. How does a believer learn to do these things? By being in communion with God through prayer, Bible reading, and practice. "Practice makes perfect" even applies to learning to obey God's Word. As we seek God's help through prayer and we practice those truths we learn from reading the Bible, it becomes easier to wait for God's direction in our life. He wants only the best for us, but it is up to each believer to accept the rest offered by Christ. As we learn to rest in Him, waiting patiently will no longer seem impossible.

Prayer

Heavenly Father, please help me to rest in You. Teach me patience as I wait for Your perfect will to be revealed…

March 12

Rest from Labor

Then I heard a voice from heaven saying to me, "Write: 'Blessed are the dead who die in the Lord from now on.'" "Yes," says the Spirit, "that they may rest from their labors, and their works follow them."

—Revelation 14:13

Service to the Lord can oftentimes be tiring, and much of the work that is done for Christ goes unnoticed. Human bodies become tired, even when our spirits want to keep going. God notices every work done in His name, my friend. There will come a time for rest and a time for recognition when our job on earth is completed. Until then, "let us not grow weary while doing good" (Galatians 6:9). God will provide you with the strength you need to continue your labors until He calls you home or returns for His Church.

Prayer

We praise You, Lord, because we know You will give us rest when You come to take us home. We will then be rewarded for all the things we have done in Your name…

March 13

Martha or Mary?

And Jesus answered and said to her, "Martha, Martha, you are worried and troubled about many things. But one thing is needed, and Mary has chosen that good part, which will not be taken away from her."

—Luke 10:41–42

This world is filled with Marthas. Marthas are organized and get things accomplished in their daily routines. They know who, what, why, when, where, and how, but do they know the important things in life?

Jesus wants us to be Marys. Marys may be slow, not quite as methodical as the Marthas, or perhaps even procrastinators, but they know what is important in life: listening to Jesus. We Marthas need to sit down, breathe deep, and listen to the Lord. There is nothing on earth more important to a believer than listening to and obeying God.

Are you a Martha or a Mary?

Prayer

Lord, open my ears so I can hear You talking to me. Please help me to really listen to Your voice and then obey. There is nothing in my life more important than You are...

March 14

Changed and Renewed

Incline your ear, and come to Me. Hear, and your soul shall live; And I will make an everlasting covenant with you—The sure mercies of David.

—Isaiah 55:3

It is God's desire that every single person receive eternal life, but not everyone inclines his or her ear to Him. Salvation comes from hearing the truth and then obeying God's call to come unto Him. God wants to cover us with His mercy and grace. When we come to know Jesus and accept His free gift of salvation, He makes a covenant with us that is everlasting. There is nothing or no one that can remove us from His hand (Romans 8:35–39).

Have you accepted the free gift of salvation, or are you just playing church? Incline your ear and listen to the living God. Today is the day of salvation—do not let it end without choosing life for your soul.

Prayer

Lord, I come to You freely, and I want life; I want to know that I will spend eternity with You. Please help me learn to hear Your voice…

March 15

Comfort One Another

The Lord God has given Me The tongue of the learned, That I should know how to speak A word in season to him who is weary. He awakens Me morning by morning, He awakens My ear To hear as the learned.

—Isaiah 50:4

It is important for believers to listen to God for more than just finding His will for their lives. We are called to encourage one another in the Lord (Hebrews 3:13). Saying just any words to someone in need is not enough—God wants us to know the right words to say to those who are tired and burdened. As we spend time with God in our daily devotions, He faithfully gives us the words necessary to encourage. We then need to follow the prompting of the Holy Spirit for His timing for when we should share those words of comfort and hope.

Prayer

Thank You, Lord, for the comfort and hope we find in You. Help us to be quick to share what we have with others…

March 16

Wonderful Peace

You will keep him in perfect peace, Whose mind is stayed on You, Because he trusts in You.

—Isaiah 26:3

Keeping one's mind focused can be a problem at times. Outside distractions interfere with our concentration. The phone ringing, the baby crying, the dryer buzzing, or other daily disturbances often interrupt our devotion and prayer time. It is important to stay focused when we are spending time with God; it is just as important to stay focused in our daily activities. A believer "whose mind is stayed on You" is living a focused life.

Everything said or done by a believer should be centered on how God wants us to respond. As we keep our minds on Christ, it becomes easier to deal with frustrations and disturbances that come our way; peace surrounds us, and we can respond in a godly way.

Prayer

Thank You for my peace, Father. When I shut the world out for a few moments to spend time with You each day, I can then handle anything that comes my way…

March 17

The Things of God

I thank God—through Jesus Christ our Lord! So then, with the mind I myself serve the law of God, but with the flesh the law of sin.

—Romans 7:25

Praise God that we become righteous through the blood of Jesus Christ, because in our flesh we can do nothing but sin. Our sin nature makes us slaves to this world. God, in His mercy, provided us with an escape plan, a way to keep our minds focused on Him: salvation through His Son, Jesus Christ. But keeping our minds on God and His law requires effort on our part. It is of the utmost importance that we maintain a daily relationship with our Lord and Savior. Bible reading, prayer, and fellowship with other believers are essential to keep us focused on the things of God. Believers need to encourage one another as well as hold one another accountable.

Do you have someone in your life who can help you keep your mind focused on the law of God?

Prayer

Lord, I thank You for the people in my life who encourage me and help me keep my life on track with You. Please use me to encourage others…

March 18

A Renewed Mind

And do not be conformed to this world, but be transformed by the renewing of your mind, that you may prove what is that good and acceptable and perfect will of God.

—Romans 12:2

Most of us would love to have a new mind, or at least one that could remember a few more things! Since that is not feasible, the renewing of our minds is the next best thing. When minds are renewed through Christ's salvation and by studying His Word, a wonderful thing happens: people are changed. Life takes on new meaning as we serve the Lord; we become transformed into children of God. It is then our desire to serve Him, seek His will, and do those things that are pleasing to Him.

We can resist the tug of the world by turning to Christ and His guidelines in the Word. How blessed we are to have a God who loves us so much that He sent His only Son to make a righteous life available to us and gave us the Bible to keep us on straight paths!

Prayer

You gave me a renewed mind, Lord. Please help me to use it to do Your will…

March 19

Gathered Together

"For where two or three are gathered together in My name, I am there in the midst of them."

—Matthew 18:20

We do not need to be in a huge church to worship God. Jesus promised the disciples that in any place where two or more were gathered together in His name, He would be there among them and hear their prayers. He does that for us today. If you are worshipping in a small church, Christ is in the middle of it; if you are worshipping in a huge church like the Cathedral of Faith, the Lord is with you. What most of us seem to forget is we—not the buildings—are the Church! As two or more gather to worship God on the Lord's Day or any other day, He is there with us.

Take time to thank God for His continual presence in your life as you worship Him this week.

Prayer

Lord, I am thankful that You don't require a large audience to hear the prayers of Your people. Thank You for those times that You have been in the midst of my small groups…

March 20

True Contentment

Likewise the soldiers asked him, saying, "And what shall we do?" So he said to them, "Do not intimidate anyone or accuse falsely, and be content with your wages."

—Luke 3:14

John the Baptist was asked by many people from different walks of life, "What shall we do?" They wanted to know how to live lives pleasing to God. John told them to give to those without clothing and food, to expect nothing more than what God gave to them, to not harm others or lie about them, and to be content with the pay received for their work (Luke 3:10–14).

Being content is perhaps the hardest directive to fulfill. We live in a land of plenty, with people always trying to keep up with the Joneses. God does not want believers to be like everyone else. He wants us to be content with what He has provided for us; He wants us to be content in Him.

What is your level of contentment today?

Prayer

Father, thank You for the earthly things You have provided for me. Help me to enjoy them fully and not take them for granted…

March 21

Godliness with Contentment

Now godliness with contentment is great gain.

—1 Timothy 6:6

The apostle Paul was writing to his beloved Timothy when he gave the exhortation to not only be godly but to be content. If a believer was able to bring godliness and contentment together, what a wonderful blessing it was!

Many believers today struggle with wanting all the extras, all the conveniences provided to us through modern technology. If we had to jump back fifty years in time and live with the conveniences provided during that era, most of us would be unable to do it. We have become so dependent on the luxuries of life that learning to be content with the necessities is almost beyond our grasp. All of the trappings of this life are temporal; reach toward those things that are eternal! Learn the truth in the words "Now godliness with contentment is great gain."

Prayer

Lord, I want to grow in You. Teach me to let go of this world and be content with Your will for my life and those things You have provided me with…

March 22

Eternal Security

Not that I speak in regard to need, for I have learned in whatever state I am, to be content.

—Philippians 4:11

It is easy to be content when life is nothing but roses, peaches, and cream. How different our attitude becomes when we are given weeds and hard biscuits. When we see others prospering while we are struggling, the last thing we want to do is be content.

Paul suffered much during his ministry: imprisonment, beatings, shipwrecks, loneliness, and other physical discomforts (2 Corinthians 11:23–29). Through it all, he remained content by maintaining a relationship with his Lord and Savior. He never forgot where God had brought him from and where he was going to spend eternity. Contentment here on earth becomes easier as we rest in our eternal security through Jesus.

Prayer

Father, please help me to not fall into the trap of covetousness. Help me be content with all You have provided for me, even when hard times come…

March 23

Eternal Values

Let your conduct be without covetousness; be content with such things as you have. For He Himself has said, "I will never leave you nor forsake you."

—Hebrews 13:5

Being raised in a large family has its pluses and minuses. The minuses were that oftentimes we did not have as many clothes in our closets as our friends; we were not able to go to dances or the movies; we did not get allowances; we never got to go on a vacation to Hawaii.

The pluses far outweighed the minuses! We were raised in the Church and surrounded by the love of not only our biological family but our church family as well. We were introduced to Jesus and His saving love. Covetousness could have easily invaded our lives if we had not had wonderful godly parents who from early on taught us what real love was all about.

I learned to be content with the things God faithfully provided for our family when they were needed; I learned that God would never leave me or forsake me (Hebrews 13:5); I learned the pluses in my life were eternal; I learned the value of having parents who loved me enough to teach me about my security in Jesus Christ; I learned those things that were true treasures.

Prayer

Thank You, Lord, for the blessings in my life…

March 24

Filled with Song

Serve the Lord with gladness; Come before His presence with singing.
—Psalm 100:2

Serving the Lord is one of the privileges, as well as joys, a believer has. As we come to understand who the person of God really is, we also come to understand how small and insignificant we are. The fact that He chose to have fellowship with us is totally awesome! Because He pulled us up from the depths of despair, we should be dancing before Him in gladness, as King David did (2 Samuel 6:14). Our hearts should be filled with songs of praise.

Circumstances often rob us of the joy of service to our Lord. That is when we need to rely on His strength to rise above the circumstances; that is when our praises should be sung from the rooftops!

Prayer

Lord, I come before You right now with a song in my heart and praise on my lips…

March 25

Give and Take

And he said: "Naked I came from my mother's womb, And naked shall I return there. The Lord gave, and the Lord has taken away; Blessed be the name of the Lord."

—Job 1:21

Contentment in the midst of suffering—how is that possible? It is only possible when one has a firm foundation to stand on. Job found his foundation—God—and stood firm on that Rock, even while God allowed Satan to strip him of everything except his life. Job never lost his faith and trust in his God. He understood that everything belongs to God and is only a temporary possession of ours to enjoy while here on earth. God gave to Job; God took away from Job. But Job always knew he had eternal life with his heavenly Father and was content with that. He knew he still had his Solid Rock to stand on, regardless of his circumstances.

Are you standing on the Solid Rock?

Prayer

Thank You, Lord, for my firm foundation. If I lost everything today, I would still have You; blessed be Your name…

March 26

Responsibility in Worship

Then Hezekiah answered and said, "Now that you have consecrated yourselves to the Lord, come near, and bring sacrifices and thank offerings into the house of the Lord." So the assembly brought in sacrifices and thank offerings, and as many as were of a willing heart brought burnt offerings.

—2 Chronicles 29:31

Accepting Jesus Christ into your heart guarantees you a place in heaven for eternity; it does not free you of responsibility for how you live your life or your service to God.

King Hezekiah told his people what they needed to do once they gave their hearts to God. Worshipping God involves sacrifice and thanksgiving. It requires offerings by a congregation as they enter into a place of worship. The Lord wants us to come and worship Him in love and in freedom, not out of obligation; we are to be responsible, not obligated.

Are you being a responsible believer?

Prayer

Salvation is free, Lord. Please help me to be responsible with the freedom I find in You…

March 27

The Great Physician

And in the thirty-ninth year of his reign, Asa became diseased in his feet, and his malady was severe; yet in his disease he did not seek the Lord, but the physicians.

—2 Chronicles 16:12

There are diseases of the spirit, the soul, the body, and the mind. It is natural to seek cures for these diseases from someone who is visible and touchable. God wants His children to do the unnatural: approach God first with the diseases in your life.

King Asa was a righteous man. God favored Asa and blessed Judah because Asa was "loyal all his days" (2 Chronicles 15:17). Yet during the end of his reign, Asa began to rely on others. He relied on the physicians to relieve him of the disease in his body. He forgot to seek the Lord to heal his disease; even righteous people tend to forget who the Great Physician is. How is your memory?

Prayer

Lord, You are truly the Healer of all hurts. Help me to remember to come to You first with the spiritual, emotional, physical, and mental diseases in my life…

March 28

Food for the Soul

Your words were found, and I ate them, And Your word was to me the joy and rejoicing of my heart; For I am called by Your name, O Lord God of hosts.

—Jeremiah 15:16

As I watch people around me living their lives without meaning or purpose, I am reminded of how much God has done for me. His Word has become the joy of my heart, because I have found my purpose in each page. I have salvation and eternal life through Jesus—the Word (John 1:1–14), the Truth, and the Life (John 14:6).

The Bible is food for our souls; as we "eat" the words written on each page, digest them, and use them for nourishment, the Lord becomes sweeter to us day by day. We cannot help but become filled with joy as we recognize how He works in our lives for the good of His Kingdom.

Prayer

Thank You, Lord, for the mercy and grace You have given to me. As I read Your Word and digest the Truth, I truly see new mercies every morning…

March 29

Swift to Hear

So then, my beloved brethren, let every man be swift to hear, slow to speak, slow to wrath.

—James 1:19

How many times do we get into trouble because we are not careful to listen yet are quick to answer? It is easy to hurt or offend someone when we allow distractions to keep us from hearing what others are really saying. A person who is hurting needs a listening ear and a loving heart. God does not want us to speak the wrong words or reply in anger because we did not correctly hear what someone was trying to say to us. As believers, we must lay aside self when someone approaches us with a concern; we must listen as God would have us listen.

The world judges God through believers. It is imperative that we try to respond as Christ would respond. Someone's salvation may depend on our listening ear and our correct response.

As you go through your day, ask God to tune your ear so that you may hear as He hears.

Prayer

Lord, I pray for a listening ear and a hearing heart. Please help me to love others as You love me and treat them with the attitude of Jesus…

March 30

Use Words Wisely

Out of the same mouth proceed blessing and cursing. My brethren, these things ought not to be so.

—James 3:10

In the book of James, believers are strongly warned about the tongue and the need for it to be controlled. The tongue is small, yet it can cause more harm than any other part of the body (James 3:5–6). James likens our tongue to a horse's bridle and a ship's helm (James 3:3–4)—both are small items that have great power to control large objects.

The words that come from our mouth can heal or they can hinder. God does not want our tongue to be "double-minded" (James 1:8). He wants only good words to come from our mouth—words that build up and edify (Ephesians 4:29). It is only through Christ's strength that a believer can control his tongue. It is important to maintain a relationship with Christ— a relationship that is growing and maturing. Only then can a believer receive the strength and wisdom to guard his tongue and use words wisely.

Prayer

Lord, my tongue belongs to You. Help me to control it through Your strength and to use words only in an edifying way...

March 31

Really Seeing God

I have heard of You by the hearing of the ear, But now my eye sees You.

—Job 42:5

Hearing about something and knowing about something are not one and the same. We hear about God through many media; whether one believes in God or not, everyone hears about Him. It is the person who has accepted Christ into his heart and invests time in building a relationship with Him who gets to know God.

Job had heard of God; he believed in God. But until his suffering, he did not know God. When everything had been stripped from him, Job spent time crying out to the Lord. In his desperate search for why, Job found God. He knew Him—really knew Him—for the first time: " But now my eye sees You."

Our knowledge of our Lord must be heart knowledge, not head knowledge. God instructs us to seek Him with our whole heart and we will find Him (Jeremiah 29:13). Invest time with God and get to know Him.

Prayer

Heavenly Father, You are the true God. I want to get to know You with my heart, not just my head…

April

April 1

Heavenly Power

For God has not given us a spirit of fear, but of power and of love and of a sound mind.

—2 Timothy 1:7

April is Earthquake Preparedness Month in California. Many organizations hold seminars during this month to inform people of what they need to do in the event of an earthquake and what supplies to have on hand. Schools and workplaces practice earthquake drills.

Although we can be mentally prepared for such a crisis, sometimes just talking about any disaster instills fear in people. Instead of being afraid, we as believers should be comforted by the knowledge that God has given us stability that others do not have; we can be secure in the power and love of Christ that belong to us. We can use this strength to keep our minds clear and free from fear—to prepare ourselves to be able to help others during a crisis.

God told Abraham, "Do not fear, for I am with you" (Genesis 26:24). This promise holds true for you today. Regardless of what calamities come your way, God is with you. Claim His promise to give you heavenly power.

Prayer

Father in heaven, I want to be fearless through You and draw from Your strength, power, and love. Please help me to live my life so that others see Your characteristics in me...

April 2

Forgive to Be Forgiven

And whenever you stand praying, if you have anything against anyone, forgive him, that your Father in heaven may also forgive you your trespasses.

—Mark 11:25

All of us want to be forgiven; many of us have trouble forgiving. It is very clear in God's Word that not being willing to forgive others hinders our relationship with God. How can we ask Him to forgive our sins when we are not willing to forgive others? God wants our human natures to become divine natures through the cleansing blood of Jesus Christ. As we remember what it cost Jesus to pay for our sins, we should be more than willing to forgive a family member, a friend, or a fellow believer of their trespasses.

God wants His fellowship with you to be unhindered. Do not let unwillingness to forgive others become a stumbling block to your spiritual growth and walk with the Lord.

Prayer

Lord, I am unworthy, but You love me anyway. Please help me to forgive others as You have forgiven me…

April 3

Sing Praises to God

Praise the Lord! I will praise the Lord with my whole heart, In the assembly of the upright and in the congregation.

—Psalm 111:1

God desires our praise. He wants us to come to Him with thanksgiving in our hearts, praising Him for who He is and for what He does in our lives. He is the Lord of creation (Psalm 33); He is the beginning and the end (Revelation 1:8); He is our shelter in the time of storm (Isaiah 25:4); He is the victor in every battle (1 John 5:4). God is God!

What a wonderful time of fellowship believers have when they gather together to praise God's name! Worshipping is a privilege and should not be looked upon as an obligation. Worship God this week freely, openly, and in the beauty of holiness.

Prayer

Today, Lord, I sing praises to Your name, with thanksgiving in my heart…

April 4

God's Riches

Command those who are rich in this present age not to be haughty, nor to trust in uncertain riches but in the living God, who gives us richly all things to enjoy.

—1 Timothy 6:17

A friend of the family called my husband one morning because he heard that a stock we owned shares in had dropped drastically in price; it had become virtually worthless. Our friend was very surprised when he did not get the reaction he expected from us—total panic. Ken and I explained that our security does not come from our retirement check, stock dividends, or any other type of earthly wealth. Our security is in our God, who promised that He will provide us with the necessary things in life: food, clothing, and shelter.

God cares for us more than for the birds and the flowers, which He cares for on a daily basis. How much more He must love us if He sent His only Son to die on the cross for our sins! Worry about my tomorrows? Not this believer!

Prayer

Thank You, my Provider and Keeper, for the gifts You bestow on me daily. May I never take Your provisions for granted and remember to give thanks every day…

April 5

A True Legacy

For I consider that the sufferings of this present time are not worthy to be compared with the glory which shall be revealed in us.

—Romans 8:18

My husband's sister Charlene died of cancer at age fifty-five. She suffered tremendously with sickness and pain as a result of the disease and the treatments. Ken watched helplessly as his baby sister struggled with every breath. Why did she have to suffer so? Couldn't God just take her and get the suffering over with?

Charlene dealt with her pain gracefully and in a dignified way, never complaining. I think she was able to do this because she knew that she was soon to be glorified—that she would be living forever with the One who made her eternity secure. Charlene's faith never wavered in those last days. Her legacy to her children is her example of tremendous faith, courage, and stamina.

Prayer

Father, none of us can know what will be required of us on this temporary journey here on earth. We do not know ahead of time what we will suffer. I ask that You give me the strength needed to help me overcome any adversity that comes into my life…

April 6

The Battle Is the Lord's

"With him is an arm of flesh; but with us is the Lord our God, to help us and to fight our battles." And the people were strengthened by the words of Hezekiah king of Judah.

—2 Chronicles 32:8

The king of Assyria was coming against the city of Judah, seeking to capture it and take control of the city and its people. In the same way, Satan is coming against every believer, seeking to steal away what belongs to God. But there is one important thing to remember in our battle against the devil: Satan, like Assyria's king, is really fighting against God. He has already lost the battle, as well as the war, and is too stubborn to realize it (Revelation 15:2)!

Be strong and faithful in the battles that come your way. Your Hero is in sight, and His name is Jesus. He will never leave you or forsake you as you go through the spiritual battles in your life (Hebrews 13:5).

Prayer

Father, all of Your children will face the snares and temptations of Satan. Please give us the strength to allow You to win those battles for us. It is in Your strength alone that we are strong and victorious...

April 7

Excuses

But they all with one accord began to make excuses.

—Luke 14:18

Jesus tells us in the book of Luke about a rich man who prepared a supper for his friends. When a servant went to invite all of those friends to his master's banquet, they made excuses why they could not attend. The excuses sound pretty weak when one reads them: have to check on land, bought an oxen, just got married (Luke 14:18–20).

Every Sunday Jesus hears excuses from His children as to why they cannot come into His house and fellowship with Him and other members of God's Kingdom. Or He hears excuses as to why we cannot lead worship, teach Sunday school, help in the nursery, or make a meal for a family in crisis. Sound familiar? Check your heart to see if what you are saying to Jesus is just an excuse. If so, enter your place of worship this week with a heart of sincerity, seek forgiveness, and enjoy true fellowship with your Master as you seek to do His will.

Prayer

Precious Lord, it truly is Your desire to have Your children at Your banquet table. If all I am offering You is excuses, please forgive me and help me be a willing participant at Your feast…

April 8

My Hand in His

The steps of a good man are ordered by the Lord, And He delights in his way. Though he fall, he shall not be utterly cast down; For the Lord upholds him with His hand.

—Psalm 37:23–24

God knows where I am going! Even though I may stumble and feel my way through the dark like a blind man at times, my Lord and Savior knows exactly where I am to be and for how long. When Satan throws a stumbling block in my path to trip me, my loving Father reaches down and pulls me up with His hand.

Sometimes I feel as if I am wandering aimlessly, but God orders even my wanderings. I don't take one step that God has not stamped "allowed" on. He takes all of my mistakes and wrong turns and puts them to good use; wrong steps taken sometimes provide the greatest lessons I learn. God continues to grow and mature me by these lessons as I clumsily make my way down life's path—my hand in His and His strength in me.

Prayer

Precious Lord, thank You for the many times You have grabbed my hand and pulled me back to safety. May I always trust in You as my Savior and Friend…

April 9

Casting Stones

So when they continued asking Him, He raised Himself up and said to them, "He who is without sin among you, let him throw a stone at her first."

—John 8:7

How quick we are to cast stones at someone else! It is much easier to see the sins others commit and to think we are "holier than thou." When a high-profile evangelist stumbles in his or her walk, people love to point fingers, wondering how "men of God" can commit such crimes against their brothers and sisters in Christ. The "bigger" the man, the harder Satan wants him to fall, because a large audience witnesses the sin and is disillusioned. We are to put no man on a pedestal! Every one of us is a sinner, redeemed only because God loved us enough to send His Son to die the death that we deserve.

The next time you are tempted to point your finger at someone or throw a stone, inspect your own life. Call on Jesus for forgiveness and for strength to clean up the areas in your life that need cleaning—before you look for someone to bruise.

Prayer

For loving me enough to die for my sins, I thank You, Jesus. May I always come quickly to You when I need forgiveness and change in my life…

April 10

Touching Others

You are our epistle written in our hearts, known and read by all men.

—2 Corinthians 3:2

I am a letter from God! People read the pages of my life and can tell by my actions if I really love the Lord. As a believer, I can touch the hearts of people I meet every day in either a positive or negative way. What a tremendous responsibility and opportunity!

My pastor, Ben Randall, once said in a sermon, "The pages of our lives get stuck together, and God can't write on them." I want every page of my life to be available to my Lord to be written on whenever He wants to give me something that He desires someone else to learn through me. I do not want the mires of life to stick my pages together!

How do our pages stay "unstuck"? We live in Christ; we commune with Him daily and read His Word; we ask Him what He wants to do with us as His instruments of communication; we live and breathe Jesus. We become living letters that touch the hearts of those around us.

Prayer

Lord, people read my life every day. May what they read be pleasing to You and have a positive influence on their lives…

April 11

Miraculous and Wonderful

And Joshua said to the people, "Sanctify yourselves, for tomorrow the Lord will do wonders among you."

—Joshua 3:5

God is a miracle-working God! It is His nature to do miraculous and wonderful things for His children. He parted the Red Sea for Moses (Exodus 14:21–22). The walls of Jericho came tumbling down for Joshua (Joshua 6:20). Noah's ark, built to God's specifications, saved Noah and his family from the flood (Genesis 6–8). The hungry lions did not devour Daniel when he was thrown into the pit (Daniel 6). As you read God's Word, the wonders go on and on.

You are reading this devotion, which to me is a wonder. I never dreamed that God would call me to write for others. It is by His providential intervention that this book has been published. When He calls us to do a job, He tells us not to worry about the finished product. He will take care of the details along the journey. May God bless you as you travel the path directed by Him.

Prayer

Father, remind me not to worry about how I will accomplish my tasks for You but to leave my journey in Your hands. You will work out all of the details if I am a faithful and obedient servant…

April 12

He Will Come

"Behold, I am coming quickly! Hold fast what you have, that no one may take your crown."

—Revelation 3:11

Are there times when you want to just throw in the towel and quit? It seems as if the more you do, the more there is to do, right? Why can't God just return and be done with it?

You are not alone if you ever feel this way. God knows that His children become weary and discouraged; Jesus experienced weariness and needed rest (John 4:6). I think that is why God tells us in Revelation 3 to not give up—to hold on tight to what we have—because He is coming back for us! That is a promise!

The next time you are weary, remember that God can be your strength. He will carry you when you can't take another step, go to another meeting, teach another class, or change another diaper. Child of God, your crown is waiting for you! Hold fast to God's promise—He will come!

Prayer

Heavenly Father, please help me to hold on to Your promises with both hands and to never let go. I know You are coming again, and I can't wait for my crown…

April 13

Always on Guard

Therefore let him who thinks he stands take heed lest he fall.

—1 Corinthians 10:12

Each believer must take great care to preserve his or her relationship with Christ. Satan would like to do nothing more than destroy those who could have the greatest impact for Christ. Jesus Himself had to be on guard against the wiles of the devil. If Christ, the perfect Lamb of God, had fallen to the temptations of Satan, there would have been no redemption for us. None of us are so strong that we do not need to daily partake of God's Word and be in communion with the One who can help us stand fast.

Do not think that you are ever "safe" from the attacks of Satan; he will not give up trying to destroy your testimony of the living Christ to the world. But take courage, believer, for God has already won the victory. Remain in Him, and you will overcome.

Prayer

Thank You for the victory I have in You, Lord. Let me never take it for granted that I am spiritually strong enough; please help me remember to daily renew my strength by fellowship with You…

April 14

Better than Silver or Gold

A good name is to be chosen rather than great riches, Loving favor rather than silver and gold.

—Proverbs 22:1

A handshake used to be enough to seal a transaction. That was during a time when men had reputations for being honest and keeping their word. Greed slowly took over as men began to stray from the teachings of God's Word.

In my lifetime alone I have seen a tremendous change toward the worship of the "almighty dollar" at the expense of men's reputations. "Seal the deal, whatever the cost" seems to be the motto of many businesses today. How sad our heavenly Father must be as He watches from on high! He sees His creation craving the things that will pass away, forgetting to nurture those things that are eternal.

Take a few moments today and check yourself: is your name worth its weight in gold?

Prayer

Please forgive me for my greed, Lord. I know that the treasures I lay up in heaven are the only ones that have true value. Help me to remember to honor my promises…

April 15

Pay Your Taxes

"Nevertheless, lest we offend them, go to the sea, cast in a hook, and take the fish that comes up first. And when you have opened its mouth, you will find a piece of money; take that and give it to them for Me and you."

—Matthew 17:27

Taxes—no one likes to pay them. We are taxed, double taxed, and even triple taxed; it doesn't seem to end. But as much as we dislike paying taxes, we are required to do so. Mark 12:17 tells us to "Render to Caesar the things that are Caesar's, and to God the things that are God's." Jesus told Peter to go and catch a fish, take the money from its mouth, and go and pay their taxes.

I'm sure if anyone could have found a way around paying taxes, Jesus could! But, He didn't; He was modeling the behavior He wanted us to follow. So the next time your taxes are due, don't grumble! Remember what Jesus demonstrated for us—pay your taxes—and let God deal with the authority!

Prayer

Heavenly Father, sometimes it is hard to obey rules that seem unfair or outrageous. But unless a rule conflicts with a command You have given us, it is our responsibility to obey. Help us to obey as graciously as Jesus did…

April 16

Lift Your Head

But You, O Lord, are a shield for me, My glory and the One who lifts up my head.

—Psalm 3:3

Being a believer does not exempt you from having down times in your life, but staying down is your choice. God wants His children to be joyful, even when faced with life's difficulties. It is only through Christ's strength that we are able to lift our heads and sing praises to God when the rug has been pulled out from under us.

King David had much going on in his life: murder, adultery, betrayal, and death. He could have remained depressed for his entire lifetime if he had not turned to God for help and deliverance. He acknowledged that it was God who lifted his head and became his glory.

Prayer

Father, You reach down into the very depths of my despair and rescue me with hope. Thank You for being faithful...

April 17

A Healthy Body

Confess your trespasses to one another, and pray for one another, that you may be healed. The effective, fervent prayer of a righteous man avails much.

—James 5:16

The life of a believer is not to be a solitary existence. Christ likens us to a body—each part depending on the other parts to work efficiently (1 Corinthians 12). We need one another. It is imperative, therefore, that we lift one another up before the throne of God. We need to fellowship with other believers so that we build relationships of trust. It is only when we come to trust in a person that we can confess to them and ask them to help us work out our shortcomings through prayer.

Just as we need to spend time alone with Christ to get to know Him, so do we need to spend time with other believers. Investing time in others requires fellowship; fellowship builds relationships; relationships build trust; trust leads to confession; confession leads to healing. Healing leads to completeness in Christ—a healthy body.

Prayer

Heavenly Father, thank You for giving us the love and support of other believers. Draw us toward You in unity and oneness of mind so that we can be a healthy body for You…

April 18

Numbered Days

So teach us to number our days, That we may gain a heart of wisdom.

—Psalm 90:12

We are not going to live in our earthly bodies forever; we have a limited time here on earth to do God's work and seek a relationship with Him. Because our time is limited, it must be used wisely. Seeking God's will and fulfilling it should be the first priority for all believers. Many of us have placed the Lord and His work at the bottom of our list of priorities. Our society has become so busy that many families no longer enjoy evening meals around a dinner table together—fast-food restaurants are flourishing! Everything we do has become a hit-and-run adventure.

Is your relationship with God and service to Him on the level of a fast-food restaurant? God desires a leisurely meal with you as you fellowship around His table. As you place Him first in your life, you will be amazed at the time you have left for everything else. You will be able to spend your time wisely.

Prayer

Lord, You are my All in All. Help me to always put You first in my life and spend the time I have on earth seeking Your wisdom…

April 19

Foolish and Unwise

"Do you thus deal with the Lord, O foolish and unwise people? Is He not your Father, who bought you? Has He not made you and established you?"

—Deuteronomy 32:6

Moses was talking to the Israelites when he asked the questions in the above Scripture. The Israelites knew God; He had shown Himself to them many times. Still, they chose to turn their backs on God over and over again.

We are still an unwise and foolish people generations later. It would seem that God's people would be the first to acknowledge Him and do Him service. Not so. Oftentimes it is believers who have known Christ the longest who take Him for granted; they do not remember the depths of sin that they were rescued from or the tribulations made easier to bear because He was at their side.

How is your memory?

Prayer

Lord, You are the same yesterday, today, and forever (Hebrews 13:8). Please forgive me for the times I have strayed from You. I do not want to be foolish and unwise…

April 20

Freely Given

Greater love has no one than this, than to lay down one's life for his friends.

—John 15:13

When push comes to shove and we are required to take a stand for Jesus, will we be faithful? Will we be like Peter, who denied Jesus three times before the rooster crowed (Matthew 26:75), or will we be like Cassie Bernall, who gave her life for Him? On April 20, 1999, in Littleton, Colorado, Cassie faced a peer who had a loaded gun in a school classroom. When asked by the gunman if she believed in God, she simply said, "Yes."[6] Cassie died that day; she willingly and boldly gave her life for her Friend, Jesus. What an awesome testimony of the faith Cassie carried with her daily!

You and I do not know the day or the hour when we will be asked to affirm or deny our faith in God. There will be no middle road; will we be willing to die for Jesus? Will we freely give our life for our Friend, as Cassie did? My prayer is that we will boldly answer "Yes."

Prayer

Father, please help me to love You enough to stand up for You even when facing death. Help me to be as bold as that young girl in Colorado; help me to be willing to die for the best Friend I will ever have—Jesus…

April 21

Created for Pleasure

You are worthy, O Lord, To receive glory and honor and power; For You created all things, And by Your will they exist and were created.

—Revelation 4:11

"What is the purpose of man?" A friend asked me that question, and I had to really think about my answer. God did create us to take care of all that He had created; He did want us to worship Him and spread the gospel of Jesus Christ. But were we created for His pleasure?

Webster's Dictionary defines pleasure as "excitement, gratification, enjoyment or happiness." It also defines it as "what one's will dictates or prefers; purpose; will; choice."[7] As I look at these definitions, I believe that we were created for God's pleasure—to do His will—to be participants in His great plan for an eternal kingdom. Yes, our Lord is worthy of glory, honor, and power. Take pleasure in Him as He takes pleasure in you.

Prayer

Thank You, Lord, for creating me to be a part of Your plan. Thank You for finding pleasure in my life…

April 22

Ready to Hear

Walk prudently when you go to the house of God; and draw near to hear rather than to give the sacrifice of fools, for they do not know that they do evil.

—Ecclesiastes 5:1

Do you enter your place of worship prepared to really hear what God has placed upon your pastor's heart? Or are you fulfilling your weekly duty to attend church, stocking up on religion for the next week? Are you worshipping out of obedience or sacrificing (grudgingly and foolishly) one of your days off to go to church?

God does not want believers to sacrifice their Sunday mornings to Him; He wants us to come and worship with our hearts prepared to hear what He is saying. God often talks to us through our spiritual leaders! A Scripture that meant nothing to us on Saturday can change our lives on Sunday because of what the Holy Spirit teaches us through our minister. Then the rest of our week should be spent drawing nearer to God.

Prayer

Lord, please help me to tune in to the lessons You want to teach me. Help me to hear and obey more than to give a foolish sacrifice (1 Samuel 15:22)…

April 23

Fiery Furnaces

If that is the case, our God whom we serve is able to deliver us from the burning fiery furnace, and He will deliver us from your hand, O king.

—Daniel 3:17

The fiery furnaces of life threaten every believer; it is not a matter of if but when you will face one. Just as God was with Shadrach, Meshach, and Abednego, He will be with you. God chose not to deliver those three godly men from the fiery furnace; He did choose to go with them through it! King Nebuchadnezzar was astonished when he saw four men in the midst of the flames (Daniel 3:24–25). Not only did God go with His servants, He protected them from any traces of the fire—not even the smell of smoke lingered on them (Daniel 3:27)!

The God of yesterday is still the God of today (Hebrews 13:8). He is faithful to protect you through the fiery furnaces of your life when you call on His name.

Prayer

Lord, thank You for being the constant in my life. I know You will be there for me when no one else can be. I praise Your name for now and ever more…

April 24

Go Therefore

"Go therefore and make disciples of all the nations, baptizing them in the name of the Father and of the Son and of the Holy Spirit, teaching them to observe all things that I have commanded you; and lo, I am with you always, even to the end of the age." Amen.

—Matthew 28:19–20

How many of us think of our homes, workplaces, and recreation centers as mission fields? God calls each believer to go out and spread the gospel, although not every believer is called to faraway places. Our family members are a daily mission field. Fellow workers are in need of God's mercy and grace, but how many of us take the time to get to know their names? Or the people in your neighborhood—how many can you call by name? The person working out next to you in the gym could be in desperate need of a friend. Are you bold enough to take the first step? God will be with you as you reach out to others and share the source of your joy.

Prayer

Heavenly Father, You are truly the joy of my life. Please help me to actively seek someone to share the gospel with today…

April 25

Full of Joy

These things I have spoken to you, that My joy may remain in you, and that your joy may be full.

—John 15:11

It is God's desire for His children to be full of joy. He does not want us to go around with long faces or to deny ourselves pleasure. The world would not be attracted to such sourpusses! But how do we become full of joy and delight in the Lord? Jesus tells us that by keeping His commandments, abiding in His love, and by loving one another we can be filled with His joy.

There will always be someone in our life who is hard to love. But God does not give us a choice: we are commanded to love others (John 15:17). When it becomes difficult to love someone due to what they have said or done, turn that person over to the Lord and pray for a forgiving heart for yourself. God will be faithful to you, and you will feel true joy as you fulfill His commands for your life.

Prayer

Father, You do not ask me to do anything that You do not equip me to do. Help me to be a faithful servant, just as You are a faithful God, and to spread Your joy to others as I teach them about Your love…

April 26

Restored Joy

Restore to me the joy of Your salvation, And uphold me by Your generous Spirit.

—Psalm 51:12

Is it possible for a believer to lose their joy? I believe it is. Many of us get caught up in the everyday trappings of life; church service becomes an obligation. We become robots, putting on fake smiles so that everyone will know that we love the Lord and are in His service. Who are we trying to fool? The Lord knows the hearts of His children; He knows when we have forgotten our first love.

In *The Plans of His Heart*, Chip Ricks says, "Those of us who were brought up in loving Christian homes sometimes find it hard to comprehend all that Jesus has done for us. We can easily be guilty of taking his sacrifice on the cross for granted."[8] I believe that taking Christ's sacrifice for granted is when we lose our joy.

Have you turned from your first love? Have you lost your joy?

Prayer

Precious Father, I thank You for the gift of salvation. When I begin to lose my joy, return my focus to the cross…

April 27

Products of Faith

For as the body without the spirit is dead, so faith without works is dead also.

—James 2:26

No one can work their way into heaven; why, then, does James tell us that our faith is dead if we do not have works? Our works are a product of our faith. We do service to God because we love Him and want Him to be our Master. God does not want our service out of obligation; He wants it out of love. Out of love we want to share Him with others. There is nothing we can do to repay Christ for His sacrifice on the cross. But, we can show our gratitude as we endeavor to further His Kingdom by joining Him in His work.

Do not be discouraged in your service to your Lord; keep your eyes focused on eternity and the glory we will one day share with our sisters and brothers in Christ.

Prayer

Father, I look forward with eager anticipation to the day that I will be with you in glory for eternity. I want others to see the fruit of the Spirit in my life until the day You return…

April 28

Serve One Another

For you, brethren, have been called to liberty; only do not use liberty as an opportunity for the flesh, but through love serve one another.

—Galatians 5:13

There is freedom in Christ. Does freedom allow us to do as we wish, knowing that we are under the law of grace? No. God's Word is very specific: we are not to continue to live our natural lives when we accept the gift of salvation; we are to live our supernatural lives to serve one another in love.

Christ gave us the greatest gift of love—His body, broken and spilled out. Every believer should be jumping at the chance to serve Him. Can you imagine what this world would be like if every believer served as God would have him or her serve?

Open your heart and allow your heavenly Father to show you how to serve those around you in love.

Prayer

Lord, You are love. Help me to live a life that reflects the person of Jesus…

April 29

Give Unto the Lord

Honor and majesty are before Him; Strength and beauty are in His sanctuary. Give to the Lord, O families of the peoples, Give to the Lord glory and strength.

—Psalm 96:6–7

What better reason could there be for corporate worship than to be in the presence of God's strength and beauty with other children of God?

Today, as I sang with the worship team at my church, my heart filled with love and my eyes brimmed with tears as I watched my sisters and brothers in Christ singing praises to our Lord! They felt it, too: the Lord's majesty, holiness, and beauty. We were in the presence of the living God!

Those who feel it is not necessary to attend church are missing out on one of the greatest blessings there is—sending up sweet incense of praise to the Lord as Christ's united Body.

Prayer

Thank You, Lord, for giving me the honor of praising You. Thank You for my brothers and sisters in the Lord who worship with me each week…

April 30

Loving Who We Are

But by the grace of God I am what I am, and His grace toward me was not in vain.

—1 Corinthians 15:10

How many of us desire to be someone other than who we are? There will always be those who appear to be wiser, prettier, richer, thinner, more knowledgeable, taller, or more talented than we are; should we desire to become that person? No. God knew exactly what He was doing when He molded each of us. He needs many different kinds of servants to perform many different tasks.

The apostle Paul recognized that God made him to be exactly who he was. Likewise, God made each of us: some to preach; some to teach; some to sing; some to tend small children; some to go to the mission field. There are no bigger or smaller servants in God's eyes. We are all equal—servants of the Lord, helping to bring about His will and His Kingdom on earth.

Whether you are changing diapers, leading worship, or evangelizing in a foreign country, you are one of God's chosen people, made in His image exactly the way He wanted you. Love who you are because He created you.

Prayer

Lord, sometimes I become dissatisfied with the person I am. Please help me to learn to love the person You made me to be and not envy others around me…

May

May 1

Equipped to Serve

But Moses said to God, "Who am I that I should go to Pharaoh, and that I should bring the children of Israel out of Egypt?"

—Exodus 3:11

Moses was astounded that God had asked him to lead the Israelites out of captivity. He felt that he was an ordinary man who was not eloquent or equipped to be a leader. Moses was reluctant to participate in the plan laid out before him, but God was persistent! He told Moses that He would be with him and give him the words that he would need (Exodus 4:11).

Many of us are reluctant to do what God has called us to do. But if we trust in God, our Creator, who made each of us unique, He will empower us to complete any task. He may not ask us to lead people out of captivity, but He will call us to serve.

Prepare your heart today to be obedient to God's will for your life.

Prayer

Father, You created me for a higher purpose; please help me to know and recognize Your plan for my life and willingly serve where I am called…

May 2

Exercise Your Gifts

As each one has received a gift, minister it to one another, as good stewards of the manifold grace of God.

—1 Peter 4:10

Spiritual gifts are given to believers to help further God's Kingdom and to encourage one another. On a wider scale, they help bring harmony, organization, and growth to the family of God. On a smaller scale, they help to build relationships with other believers so that we can encourage and pray for one another.

Whether our gifts are used or not determines if the growth in our churches is healthy and balanced. In our physical bodies, if a part is not continually exercised it becomes weak and may even stop functioning altogether. Our spiritual gifts, if not used, also become weak and ineffective. Not using the gifts He has given us saddens the Lord; He gave them to us to be used wisely and not wasted. Being a good steward of our gifts should be a priority for each believer.

Prayer

Thank You, Lord, for the gift of encouragement You have given to me. Help me to use it to lift others when they need an encouraging word or a hug…

May 3

No Handicaps

Do not neglect the gift that is in you, which was given to you by prophecy with the laying on of the hands of the eldership.

—1 Timothy 4:14

Each believer is equipped with at least one spiritual gift. God gave us our gifts to be used in ministry. To not use a gift is like amputating a hand, foot, arm, or leg from the body. A body works at maximum efficiency when all of its parts are working properly. You can learn to function without a body part, but your capacity to perform certain duties will be limited. God desires a body that has no amputated parts; as He is perfect, He seeks to perfect His Church. When each believer exercises his or her gifts, the body becomes unified and works in a synchronized way, perfecting and edifying the saints.

Allow God to use you in perfecting His Body. Do not allow your unused gifts to become a disability.

Prayer

Lord, I am a part of Your Body. Please help me to use the gifts You have given to me, so that I do not hinder Your work…

May 4

Knowledge Comes with Risk

But he who did not know, yet committed things deserving of stripes, shall be beaten with few. For everyone to whom much is given, from him much will be required; and to whom much has been committed, of him they will ask the more.

—Luke 12:48

Did you ever stop to think that the knowledge you have regarding God's truth comes with risk? Knowledge comes with the risk of being held more accountable to your Lord and Savior Jesus Christ! Wow—that is enough to make some people stop seeking a better understanding of God's Word. Maybe that is why Jesus said, "Because narrow is the gate and difficult is the way which leads to life, and there are few who find it" (Matthew 7:14).

Giving your heart to Christ and wanting to grow in Him comes with great responsibility. It is a commitment and requires a change in lifestyle; it requires growing in the Word and becoming accountable. How much of a risk taker are you?

Prayer

Heavenly Father, the knowledge I receive from You is precious. Help me to use it wisely so that I may grow in You and share Your truth with others…

May 5

Come with Boldness

Therefore, brethren, having boldness to enter the Holiest by the blood of Jesus, by a new and living way which He consecrated for us, through the veil, that is, His flesh.

—Hebrews 10:19–20

Christians are to be bold when entering into the Holy of Holies. We received permission to go directly to the throne of God when Christ became our High Priest through His crucifixion on the cross. Yet many of us are still timid when approaching God. We are not reconciled to the fact that the God of Creation is also our Abba—our daddy, in today's English (Romans 8:15). God wants us to be confident in our faith. He will always be there for us whenever we cry out to Him. He is an eternal God who rewards those who exercise boldness and confidence in Christ.

Prayer

Abba, Father, please help me to be bold and confident when I approach Your throne. You have promised that I can come to You with every need. Thank You for being my daddy…

May 6

Verbal Communication

That the sharing of your faith may become effective by the acknowledgment of every good thing which is in you in Christ Jesus.

—Philemon 1:6

Worshipping God as a corporate body of believers is a way of sharing all the good things that God does for us and gives to us. Our faith grows when we hear of God's faithfulness to others, and through their encouragement we receive strength to help us carry on. It is often the hug and verbal support a fellow Christian offers that allow us to take steps of faith. By hearing, faith grows (Romans 10:17). You, as a part of your church, are participating in God's plan for the fellowship of believers and the building of faith.

Prayer

Lord, You live in me. Help me to share You with others so that by hearing they might believe…

May 7

Displeased with Complaints

Now when the people complained, it displeased the Lord.

—Numbers 11:1

The Israelites were great complainers during their exodus from Egypt. Instead of remembering how faithful God had been to them by delivering them out of bondage and meeting their needs, they complained about what they did not have. They even went to the point of wishing that they were back in Egypt (Numbers 14:2–4)! How ungrateful they must have seemed to their heavenly Father.

We believers today are not very different. We complain all the time about situations in our lives, things we do not have (and probably do not need!), and that God is not there when we really need Him. As parents, we know how we feel when our children complain instead of being thankful for what we have provided for them. Is God so different that, as our parent, He should not feel hurt or disappointment when we act toward Him as our children do toward us? Yes, God is displeased with our complaints; are you a complainer?

Prayer

Lord, I ask Your forgiveness for the complaining I do in my life. You have faithfully provided for my every need, and I have never had to do without the necessities…

May 8

A Proverbs 31 Mom

Who can find a virtuous wife? For her worth is far above rubies. Her children rise up and call her blessed; her husband also, and he praises her.

—Proverbs 31:10, 28

An ancient Jewish proverb says, "God could not be everywhere, and therefore He made mothers."[9] As a believer, I know that God can be everywhere, but I find it touching that He chose women to nurture His little ones. How blessed the children are who are raised in a godly home with a "Proverbs 31" mother!

If you are a mom, do not take your role lightly—God has given you an awesome responsibility. Ask Him to help you teach your children in the way they should go. He will give you strength when you feel there is none left. He has promised to never leave you or forsake you (Hebrews 13:5), especially when you are watching over His children. God will help you be the best mom possible; you can be a "Proverbs 31" mom.

Prayer

Lord, thank You for mothers. They are the nurturers of Your precious little ones. Please give them strength, wisdom, and love to help them in their daily struggles…

_____
_____
_____
_____
_____
_____

Morning and Evening

To stand every morning to thank and praise the Lord, and likewise at evening.

—1 Chronicles 23:30

The Levites were the ones chosen by God to stand between Him and the Israelites. It was their job to bring the sacrifices before the Lord and to thank and praise Him on behalf of the people.

When Christ died on the cross, an intercessor was no longer needed; He became our High Priest (Hebrews 5:10). The responsibility now falls on every believer to go to the Lord personally with praise and thanks and to ask for forgiveness of sins. But it is easy to become busy with our daily activities and forget our morning and evening quiet times with Jesus.

We rob ourselves of God's full blessings when we neglect our daily devotions. Time spent alone with our heavenly Father should be the first and the last thing we do each day.

Prayer

Heavenly Father, help me to remain steadfast in You and to give thanks in all things from morning to night…

May 10

Look Beyond Our Circumstances

Sing praises to the Lord, who dwells in Zion! Declare His deeds among the people.

—Psalm 9:11

The Lord deserves our praise every day. Sometimes what He gets is not what He deserves. If we wake up grouchy, we forget to praise God; if we are not feeling well, we forget to praise God; if we have a task to complete that we are dreading, we forget to praise God. God never forgets us!

King David learned to praise God in the bad times as well as in the good. He suffered numerous tragedies, yet he wrote many of the beautiful songs of praise in the *Book of Psalms*. David learned to look beyond his circumstances—to see the glory of his God in all things. Oh, that we could all be like David and learn to look beyond our circumstances and glorify our Lord in everything!

Prayer

Father, You never forget Your children. Please help me to never forget You and to praise Your name before all people…

May 11

Worthy of Praise

Rejoice in the Lord, O you righteous! For praise from the upright is beautiful.

—Psalm 33:1

The Lord is worthy of praise. Part of our righteousness—our right relationship with Christ—is based on praise. It is during praise that we can open our hearts and thank God for the love He bestows on us daily. Praise helps prepare our hearts and minds for worship. As we sing our praises, we are sending up sweet incense to the Lord. Our hearts can enter into worship in an intimate way. Who can stay depressed when they are singing God's praises! As the Father looks down on His children praising their God, He smiles upon us and meets us right where we are.

Prayer

Lord, I praise You for who You are. I am unworthy of Your love, yet You daily work in my life to form me into the image of Your Son…

May 12

Voice Your Joy

The voice of rejoicing and salvation Is in the tents of the righteous; The right hand of the Lord does valiantly.

—Psalm 118:15

When something is voiced, it is spoken audibly, so that others can hear. The joy of our salvation should be voiced so that others can know how the Lord is changing our lives. Rejoicing is a part of the corporate worship shared by believers. Sometimes we forget the uniqueness of our relationship with Christ. As we share with others, we are reminded of how awesome God really is.

If worshipping and sharing with other believers is not a part of your life because you find it hard to voice your salvation, how can you possibly share the gospel with sinners living in a world ruled by Satan?

Prayer

Lord, please give me the boldness I need to share You with others. Help me to be very vocal when it comes to sharing how You have touched and changed my life…

May 13

Free in Christ

Enter into His gates with thanksgiving, And into His courts with praise. Be thankful to Him, and bless His name.

—Psalm 100:4

Every Sunday, believers enter into the gates and courts of our Lord. We go to our places of worship to give thanks to God for His mercy and grace. We go to praise Him for His unfailing love. How we praise God should be determined by how He directs us, not by how we think others want us to express praise. We are free in Christ to be who He wants us to be and to praise in the freedom He has given to us.

Look deep into your heart and ask God how He wants you to worship Him as you enter your place of worship this week. Then act in obedience as you praise His name freely and thankfully.

Prayer

Father God, You created each of us uniquely. Help us to use that uniqueness to bring glory to Your name through our freedom in Christ…

May 14

God or Man?

And the Lord said to Samuel, "Heed the voice of the people in all that they say to you; for they have not rejected you, but they have rejected Me, that I should not reign over them."

—1 Samuel 8:7

How like the Israelites we Christians have become! We have spiritual leaders who are godly, as Samuel was, but they are preaching something that we are not comfortable hearing. So we gravitate toward those who will tell us what we want to hear; we cry, "Give us a king to judge us" (1 Samuel 8:6). We cling to the values that fall in line with the "politically correct" instead of clinging to God's values.

God does not necessarily want us to be popular; He wants us to be obedient. King Saul wanted to be popular, so instead of being the king that God desired him to be, he bowed down to the people. As a result, God took away Saul's power and peace.

If you and I are not careful about whom we choose to please—God or man—the Lord can take away our effectiveness in ministry and the peace that comes from obedience. Joshua's words "Choose for yourselves this day whom you will serve" (Joshua 24:15) apply to us today. Will we serve the God of Abraham, as Joshua chose to do, or bow down to the people?

Prayer

Lord, You are the true King. May I always bow down to Your righteous authority and not to the pressure of my peers…

May 15

A Living Example

As for you, my son Solomon, know the God of your father, and serve Him with a loyal heart and with a willing mind; for the Lord searches all hearts and understands all the intent of the thoughts. If you seek Him, He will be found by you; but if you forsake Him, He will cast you off forever.

—1 Chronicles 28:9

King David gave his son Solomon the best legacy and advice a father could give to a child: live for God with all your heart! In spite of some wrong choices, David was known as "*a man after His [God's] own heart*" (1 Samuel 13:14).

Many times, we as parents tell our children how we want them to live and give them our rules. But we do not want to live by the same set of standards; we become "do as I say and not as I do" parents. Our children need to see our obedience to the Lord; they need to see us serve Him with perfect hearts and willing minds. As David was a living example of wholeheartedly seeking after God, so should we be. Actions really do speak louder than words; what do you want your children to see?

Prayer

Lord, I do not want to hinder my children by my wrong actions. Please help me to live every day in the way I want my children to live…

_____
_____
_____
_____
_____
_____

Humbled Before God

"I tell you, this man went down to his house justified rather than the other; for everyone who exalts himself will be humbled, and he who humbles himself will be exalted."

—Luke 18:14

Pride: man's number one enemy. Everyone knows the old saying "Pride goeth before a fall." Those words actually come from God's Word. Proverbs 16:18 says, "Pride goes before destruction, And a haughty spirit before a fall." God wants us to lean on Him, but often our pride tells us we do not need anyone other than ourselves. As quickly as we can be puffed up in ourselves, God can deflate us. Only when we realize our position in Christ and become humble in spirit can God use us. When we set aside pride, God will lift us up and then use us for His glory.

Prayer

Father, I do not want to be a proud and boastful person. Please give me a spirit of humbleness so that I may serve You well...

May 17

Spiritually Minded

For to be carnally minded is death, but to be spiritually minded is life and peace.

—Romans 8:6

People are running around in increasing numbers like chickens with their heads cut off. I was raised in the country and many times witnessed a chicken being prepared for dinner. After its head was severed with a hatchet or an ax, the chicken would run and flop around, wings flapping everywhere. That apparent sign of life was all reflex action—the chicken was already dead, but didn't know it.

When our minds are not focused on God, we tend to run in all directions. We are looking for something we cannot quite put our finger on. God tells us to "Be still, and know that I am God" (Psalm 46:10). Our heavenly Father does not want us running aimlessly around during our time here on earth; He has given us instruction in the Word so that we have a road map for a life of peace.

Prayer

Precious Lord, help me to slow down long enough to listen and hear You as You give direction to me. Keep my mind focused on the things of God and not of man…

May 18

Faithfulness and Truth

O Lord, You are my God. I will exalt You, I will praise Your name, For You have done wonderful things; Your counsels of old are faithfulness and truth.

—Isaiah 25:1

God is faithful. When times of trial and hardship come upon us, we tend to forget this. We forget the saints God was faithful to, the "cloud of witnesses" (Hebrews 12:1) that we read about in His Word. God gave Abraham his promised son, Isaac (Genesis 21:1–3); Noah was saved from the flood (Genesis 8:18); Joseph became great in the land of Egypt (Genesis 42:6); Pharaoh's daughter saved Moses from death (Exodus 2:1–10). There are many more examples of God's faithfulness.

By reading the Bible daily and walking in a right relationship with Christ, we can be lifted up when we are down. God never changes. He will be the same today as He was yesterday. God will be as faithful to you in your circumstances as He was to the great heroes of the Bible. Put your faith in Him and rest on His promises.

Prayer

Heavenly Father, sometimes I forget that You are a God whose truth never changes. When I become forgetful, please remind me of that truth…

Great Is Your Reward

"But you, be strong and do not let your hands be weak, for your work shall be rewarded!"

—2 Chronicles 15:7

It is easy to become discouraged when doing the Lord's work. There are times you spend hours preparing a lesson for a class and no one shows up. Your pastor may spend a whole week preparing a sermon on salvation and no one comes forward during the altar call. You raise your children in the Lord, but they turn from Him when they leave the nest.

Why spend so much time and energy performing a task when no one seems to notice or care? Because God cares. He sees everything we do and hears every word that comes out of our mouths. He reminds us to be patient—our reward will come. In a society that wants instant gratification, waiting is hard. But God tells us, "Great is your reward in heaven" (Matthew 5:12). Be patient, my friend; your reward will be worth it all!

Prayer

Father, there are times when I just want to give up. Please help me continue to run the race because You are there waiting for me at the finish line…

May 20

Wholly and Joyfully

Then the people rejoiced, for they had offered willingly, because with a loyal heart they had offered willingly to the Lord; and King David also rejoiced greatly.

—1 Chronicles 29:9

Sunday, the Lord's Day, is a day to rejoice. It is a day to offer praise to God for what He has done in you and for you. Sunday is a day to place God before everyone and everything as you worship and adore Him.

Do you, as a believer, look forward to the day set aside to worship our Lord and Savior? Or do you wake up wishing you could go back to bed because it is your only day to sleep in? Christ did not sleep in when He knew He was going to die on the cross for your sins; He did not sleep in when He folded His death shroud and exited His grave; He is not sleeping in as He sits at the right hand of God, making intercession for you; He will not be sleeping in when He returns for His own.

Worship the Lord this week with "a loyal heart" and offer your gifts to the Lord willingly. He alone is worthy of all you can give. Give with great joy!

Prayer

Lord, thank You for all You have done for me. Help me to always be grateful enough to worship You wholly and joyfully…

May 21

As Little Children

But Jesus said, "Let the little children come to Me, and do not forbid them; for of such is the kingdom of heaven."

—Matthew 19:14

A friend came to me wanting to know if I could explain the Bible to her in simple terms. She apologized for being an uneducated person and asked if it would be too much trouble for me to help her. I had to remind her that God wants us all to come to Him simply, as little children.

Sometimes our education gets in the way of the simplicity of God's Word and its message. It would help us "educated" believers tremendously to come down to a child's level once in a while. We would be reminded that children of God come in all sizes, shapes, and ages, with different backgrounds and educations.

Woe unto those who hurt one of God's little ones or turn away from the needs and cries of their hearts (Matthew 18:6)! If children come to you—whether they are five or fifty-five—reach out and embrace them as Jesus does.

Prayer

Lord, please remind me to have the faith of a little child. Your Kingdom is made up of such little ones, and I desire to be a part of that Kingdom…

A Shining Light

Let your light so shine before men, that they may see your good works and glorify your Father in heaven.

—Matthew 5:16

"This little light of mine, I'm gonna let it shine…" Remember singing that chorus in Sunday school? It was much easier to let our light shine and not hide it under a bushel when we were small children. Unfortunately, as we grow up, most of us tend to be less open about the light that shines within us—Jesus Christ. We care more about what others think than we do about being doers of the Word. God wants us to be bright lights in this world and bring glory to His name! People should be able to see Jesus in us by everything we say and do. It should not matter to believers what other people think.

Today you have a choice: will you let your light shine so that others can see Jesus, or will you hide your light under a bushel so that it is hidden?

Prayer

Precious Lord, I want to be a ray of light to those who are in darkness. Please give me the love and courage I need to spread Your Word by letting my light shine for You…

May 23

A Servant's Heart

And whoever desires to be first among you, let him be your slave—just as the Son of Man did not come to be served, but to serve, and to give His life a ransom for many.

—Matthew 20:27–28

Human beings are basically selfish. We are of the mentality that our needs are more important than the needs of others. Not so. The Word of God tells us that even Jesus came to take care of the needs of others, placing their needs before His own.

Serving the Lord is not easy. It means allowing Christ to work through us even when a situation is tough and seems to be beyond our abilities to deal with it. When God calls us, He equips us. It is our responsibility, as children of the Lord, to have such a personal relationship with Him that we not only hear God's call to serve, we also ask for His help in preparing for that service. God is faithful to give when we ask: "Ask, and it will be given to you" (Matthew 7:7). Ask Him to give you a servant's heart.

Prayer

Heavenly Father, thank You for the privilege of serving others in Your name. You are truly Servant of all servants, King of all kings, and Lord of all lords…

May 24

Strong to Destruction

But when he was strong his heart was lifted up, to his destruction, for he transgressed against the Lord his God by entering the temple of the Lord to burn incense on the altar of incense.

—2 Chronicles 26:16

King Uzziah initially depended on the Lord to help him build back the kingdom. God gave him the strength to win battles and fortify Jerusalem. Uzziah's army grew and his herds prospered. He became strong; he became proud.

Uzziah lost patience one day and entered the temple to do what only the priests were ordained to do: burn incense upon the altar. So serious was this offense that Uzziah immediately broke out in leprous spots. The Lord made Uzziah pay for his transgression, and "he was cut off from the house of the Lord" (2 Chronicles 26:21). When we no longer think we need God on a daily basis, He can cut us off from His blessings.

Prayer

Heavenly Father, I need You in my life every day. Please protect me from pride so that I do not turn my back on You and try to do things on my own…

May 25

Do It As Unto Me

"And the King will answer and say to them, 'Assuredly I say to you, inasmuch as you did it to one of the least of these My brethren, you did it to Me.'"

—Matthew 25:40

Our church secretary's mother was about to lose her home. Due to a stroke, this elderly woman could no longer work; therefore, she could not pay her mortgage. A reverse mortgage would be the answer to her problem. After an appraisal, the bank said that the loan could be approved if $14,000 worth of repairs were made. Since the family did not have the money to make the repairs, the need was brought before the church congregation.

The members rose to the call. One hundred men and thirty-two women volunteered their time to put on a new roof, repair dry-rotted wood, replace dry wall, paint, lay new linoleum and carpet, and prepare meals for the workers. Many of these volunteers did not know the elderly woman in need; they only knew that a sister in Christ needed help.

What a testimony to the community! God's people pulled together in a time of crisis. Their only reward would be in knowing that Jesus saw them answer the call "inasmuch as you did it to one of the least of these My brethren, you did it to Me."

Prayer

Lord, please open my eyes so that I may see those in need around me. What I do for others, I am doing for You…

May 26

Living Love Letters

You are our epistle written in our hearts, known and read by all men; clearly you are an epistle of Christ, ministered by us, written not with ink but by the Spirit of the living God, not on tablets of stone but on tablets of flesh, that is, of the heart.

—2 Corinthians 3:2–3

The life of a believer is a letter from Christ written to everyone. Once we have accepted Christ as our personal Savior, the Holy Spirit is free to write on our hearts and fill out the blank pages of our lives. What a worthy honor—to become parchment paper for the Finger of God!

If we allow Him to, Christ can reveal wonderful things to us through His Spirit. In God's Word, we are told that His thoughts and ways are not ours (Isaiah 55:8–9). He has plans for us that we simply cannot understand!

What better way is there for us to express our gratitude to Christ for dying on the cross for our sins than to allow our lives to be read by others? Let your life be an open book so the world can see what God has written on the pages of your life.

Prayer

Father God, what a privilege it is to be chosen for service to You. May the open pages of my life tell a story of love, redemption, and hope…

May 27

Daily Worship

"Our fathers worshiped on this mountain, and you Jews say that in Jerusalem is the place where one ought to worship."

—John 4:20

Worship should take place on a daily basis and in our hearts. God is no longer dwelling in a building or city; God dwells in the hearts of believers. If we only worship God on Sunday morning, we are robbing ourselves of the most precious relationship we can have. God wants you to seek Him "with all your heart, with all your soul, and with all your mind" (Matthew 22:37). Finding God is most effective when it is done every single day, including Sunday.

When you worship in your church this week, do not leave your faith there. Take it with you and grow closer to Christ each day as you allow the Lord to take first place in your life.

Prayer

Lord, I do not want to place You on a shelf Monday through Saturday as some do with the Bible, using it only on Sunday. I want You to be in my life every minute of every day…

May 28

First Place

My voice You shall hear in the morning, O Lord; In the morning I will direct it to You, And I will look up.

—Psalm 5:3

No phones ringing. No neighbors knocking on the door. No grandchildren running around my feet, demanding my attention: the perfect time to spend with God.

It is 4:30 in the morning, and I have just returned from dropping my husband off at the car pool. I now have two choices: I can go back to bed or I can start my day with God. Nine times out of ten, I opt for the second choice. I've found that when I start my day by reading God's Word and sending up praises, my day runs more smoothly.

God loves to hear from us before we are distracted by the daily chores we must tackle each day. When God has first place in our life, everything else falls into place. Yes, 4:30 a.m. is the perfect time to start my day with God. When is your perfect time?

Prayer

Lord, I love You. Thank You for each day that is given to me. Please remind me to start my day with You, putting You before everything else…

May 29

Seek Him Early

I love them that love me; and those that seek me early shall find me.
—Proverbs 8:17, KJV

God's Word tells us that if we seek Him early we will find Him. But what does early mean in this context? In *Strong's Concordance,* we find the Hebrew word for early is *shâchar.* It means to "be (up) early at any task; seek diligently in the morning."[10] We should seek God diligently and with all our heart.

To me, this verse also means that we should seek God early in our lives. When I think of all the wasted years that I spent seeking after worldly things, it breaks my heart. I accepted Christ as my Savior at twelve years of age. I did not seek God with my whole heart until I was thirty-seven. What a waste! I urge you to seek God diligently—in the morning and in your years—and watch the wonderful way He molds and shapes you into what He desires you to be.

Prayer

Father God, I want to be molded into what You desire me to be. Help me to seek You early and wholeheartedly...

May 30

Appointed by God

Let every soul be subject to the governing authorities. For there is no authority except from God, and the authorities that exist are appointed by God.

—Romans 13:1

It is easy to criticize or belittle our government officials. We see America slipping farther and farther away from being "one nation under God." We cannot always understand why God allows these leaders to be in power, but He does. In fact, God appoints these leaders.

In Isaiah we read that God's thoughts are not our thoughts and God's ways are not our ways. He knows what He wants to happen, and He places people in positions of authority to bring it about.

Memorial Day is the perfect time to remember those in authority and the many men and women who have given their lives for their country in obedience to that authority. In memory of them and their sacrifices, I urge you to pray for the leaders of our country. Pray that they will seek guidance from above and that America will once again be united under God.

Prayer

Precious Lord, thank You for the people who have willingly given their lives for their country. May we never forget that we have our freedom because someone paid a price. Please be with the leaders of our country and draw them to You…

May 31

Ignorance Is Not Bliss

Because you have forgotten the law of your God, I also will forget your children.

—Hosea 4:6

Newspapers and television news segments are full of depressing stories about children. Children are killing each other because of jealousy, drugs, or alcohol. Children are turning on their parents because they no longer see them as authority figures and don't want to be told what to do. Gangs are increasing in number because of broken homes. Children need to belong to a family; the gang becomes their family. Is it any wonder we are seeing this increase in adolescent violence when we, as parents, are spending less time teaching our children godly principles?

We must instill God's law on the hearts and in the minds of our children while they are young. If we do not provide them with the tools they need to learn how to live a righteous life, we become guilty of forgetting the knowledge of God and run the risk of God forgetting our children; He will give them up to the immorality of this world (Romans 1:28). Are you willing to pay that price?

Prayer

Lord, ignorance of Your Word separates me from You. Please forgive me and help me to learn Your ways. Remind me to teach Your law to my children and grandchildren…

June

June 1

God's Strength

It is God who arms me with strength, And makes my way perfect.

—Psalm 18:32

At one time in her life, Joni Eareckson Tada wanted to commit suicide. I heard her testimony on "Focus on the Family" radio while driving one day. Suicide! This great woman of God wanted to end her life when, at the age of seventeen, she became confined to a wheelchair because of a diving accident. From that day forward, all of her physical needs would have to be met by others. How did Joni overcome the desire to end her life? She asked for God's strength; she asked for Christ to live through her and help her face each day in His strength.

Joni has a marvelous ministry today. She paints, writes books, sings, has a wheelchair ministry, and even goes on speaking tours. But if it had not been for God's strength, Joni would have given up on life. This dynamic woman has become a living testimony to others of how we can overcome anything through God's power.

What disability do you have? Is it physical, emotional, or spiritual? Allow God to help you overcome your weakness and live a life of victory through Him.

Prayer

Precious Lord, I ask today that You become my strength. Through You, I can do all things...

June 2

Walk the Talk

My little children, let us not love in word or in tongue, but in deed and in truth.

—1 John 3:18

How many times have we heard the statement "You'd better walk the talk"? These words are in accordance with God's Word. We are told to love others by our actions, not just by the words that roll off our tongues almost without thought. When we tell our children we love them, do we follow through with a kiss or a hug? How many believers claim to love the Lord, yet they neglect to spend time with Him in prayer and Bible reading?

God wants us to back up everything we say with everything we do. Will we mess up? You bet! But God will lovingly pick us up, forgive us, and continue to be by our side. As we spend more time getting to know Jesus, it becomes easier to back up our words with actions.

Prayer

Father, I want everything I do to be a reflection of what I say. Please help me to show Your love to others by being a "walker" and not just a "talker"…

June 3

On His Shoulders

But those who wait on the Lord Shall renew their strength; They shall mount up with wings like eagles, They shall run and not be weary, They shall walk and not faint.

—Isaiah 40:31

I cannot take another step. I cannot do one more chore. I cannot find the energy to serve. A still small voice inside quietly says, "Yes, you can. Rely on My strength and not your own. I can carry you and share your burden. Rest in Me."

Every believer has been too tired or too discouraged at some point in his or her Christian walk. It is Christ alone who can carry us past the "I cannot" to become soaring eagles! His strength is what allows us to put one foot in front of the other and continue down the rough roads of life. His strength is what allows us to say, "I can do all things through Christ who strengthens me" (Philippians 4:13).

Prayer

Precious Lord, when I cannot go another step, remind me to let You carry me on Your shoulders. Your strength will take me where I need to go…

June 4

Either Or—Not Both

You cannot drink the cup of the Lord and the cup of demons; you cannot partake of the Lord's table and of the table of demons.

—1 Corinthians 10:21

We have all seen this scene in gangster movies: The Mafia has a hit man who is hired to kill someone; after the person is taken out, the hit man is paid and goes on to a new target. This scene continues during the week until Sunday rolls around. Then the hit man, who is a churchgoer, attends church, confesses to the priest, does his penance, walks out the door of the church, and is as happy as a lark because he is okay with God—the priest told him so! Monday comes around and the hit man is out killing again. To me, this is trying to drink of the Lord's table and the devil's table. God says this cannot be.

Is a Christian who goes to church on Sunday and then lives his or her life the way they want the rest of the week any different from the hit man? We are to live for Christ every day, and when we commit a sin, we are to ask for forgiveness with a heart of repentance. True repentance requires that we turn away from our sin.

Perhaps there is something in your life that requires forgiveness. Ask God to give you a heart of repentance and a desire to live for Him alone.

Prayer

Heavenly Father, You are the Master of my life. Please help me to resist Satan daily and not be tricked into drinking from his table…

June 5

Not Ashamed of Jesus

O my God, I trust in You; Let me not be ashamed; Let not my enemies triumph over me.

—Psalm 25:2

Sometimes it is harder to proclaim Christ among friends than among enemies. I have a friend whom I have tried to be a witness to for twenty-one years. Many times I have found myself hesitating when I wanted to talk about the Bible or church activities. Why? I was not ashamed of my God. What was I afraid of? Rejection. I did not want to be rejected by my friend because of my faith. I had to ask God to help me overcome this fear and daily put my trust in Him. As a result, my friend now talks about the Bible and even asks to attend certain church activities. It has been a long twenty-one years. But God is softening my friend's heart because I have allowed Him to help me overcome my fear and I am not ashamed of my Jesus.

Prayer

Precious Jesus, You were not ashamed of me when You died on the cross for my sins. I do not want to be ashamed or embarrassed to share You with others…

June 6

Through the Fire

You have caused men to ride over our heads; We went through fire and through water; But You brought us out to rich fulfillment.

—Psalm 66:12

Praise God that He goes with us through the fires and floods of life! When I become discouraged, I remember the stories of Shadrach, Meshach, and Abednego as they went through the fiery furnace (Daniel 3:25) and Noah surviving the flood (Genesis 7). God protected them through their trials and was with them.

The fires in our life are disease, divorce, loss of material possessions or jobs, and persecution because of our faith. Whether or not we ever go through a physical fire is irrelevant; whatever we go through, God will go with us. He has promised to never leave us (Joshua 1:5), regardless of our circumstances. When we put our faith in the God of promise, we can live in the freedom of His grace and protection.

Prayer

Lord, thank You that Your promises are true. I can read Your Word and learn of Your faithfulness to the saints of the past and know that You are the same today…

June 7

Unequally Yoked

Do not be unequally yoked together with unbelievers. For what fellowship has righteousness with lawlessness? And what communion has light with darkness?

—2 Corinthians 6:14

"What does unequally yoked mean to you?" When asked that question by my pastor, I responded as most believers would: Do not marry an unbeliever. But being unequally yoked encompasses much more than the marriage arena. We should apply this verse in Corinthians to every aspect of our lives. We must be careful whom we choose as business partners; our best friends and counselors should be believers; the churches we attend should teach sound doctrine and not compromise the truth of God's law. Every area of our life needs to be evaluated by the equally yoked principle found in God's Word.

King Solomon, the wisest man on earth, became unequally yoked with unbelieving wives, which led to his heart being turned away from God (1 Kings 11:1–3). One cannot go against God's wise counsel and come out a winner.

Who are you unequally yoked with in your life that could lead to your downfall?

Prayer

Lord, I need to remember that the wise words of Your counsel are for my good, not for my destruction. Please give me ears to hear and a willing heart to obey the words of Your mouth…

_____

_____

_____

_____

_____

_____

June 8

Quiet Places

Now it came to pass, as He was praying in a certain place, when He ceased, that one of His disciples said to Him, "Lord, teach us to pray, as John also taught his disciples."

—Luke 11:1

When the Scriptures mention Jesus praying "in a certain place," one automatically assumes that it is a quiet place. I would never have guessed that my certain place would be in the middle of Chicago's O'Hare International Airport!

I had been praying for some quiet time alone with the Lord—away from all of the distractions that daily come my way as I babysit my two little grandchildren. Well, Hurricane Floyd saw to it that I got stranded in Chicago for over twenty-four hours during a trip to visit my family in New Jersey. In the midst of all the hustle and bustle, I actually found peace and quiet!

When we are in true fellowship with our Lord, He can bring us to a quiet place even in the midst of chaos. A hurricane provided me with the time I had prayed for.

Prayer

Lord, thank You for the quiet that You give to my spirit in the middle of my storms...

June 9

His Best, Not Ours

"For My thoughts are not your thoughts, Nor are your ways My ways," says the Lord. "For as the heavens are higher than the earth, So are My ways higher than your ways, And My thoughts than your thoughts."

—Isaiah 55:8–9

God tells us to trust Him with all our heart (Proverbs 3:5) because He is the Beginning and the End (Revelation 21:6). Period. He works in ways that we cannot comprehend. Many times, believers do not realize that God has been working in their lives until a situation is over. Looking back, we can see that His hand was guiding us all along.

There have been times when I wanted something very much but God said, "No," and I reluctantly complied. As time went by, I was thankful that God knew what was down the road for me when He told me no.

God wants His best for His children; often, His no is best for us. We must trust God and wait with eager anticipation as we watch His plan for us unfold.

Prayer

Just as a loving father wants the best for his children here on earth, Lord, You want the best for me. Please help me to receive even the "no" answers You have for me with a heart of thanksgiving…

Minister to Others

"For even the Son of Man did not come to be served, but to serve, and to give His life a ransom for many."

—Mark 10:45

Sunday is a day for believers to go to church, get fed, and then go on with the rest of their week, forgetting to think about God until the next Sunday. Church is church, after all—you just do it, right? Well, God's idea of church is about more than Sunday.

Sunday is our day of worship, but Monday through Saturday we need to take the Church to the streets and minister to those in need around us. It may mean just being a friend to a lonely, elderly woman who is stranded with you in an airport. I was given this opportunity while on a trip and received a true blessing through the woman's gratitude and our conversation.

Lonely people are not just in airports, though; many lonely people live in our neighborhoods, and we do not even realize it. It is time to take the blinders off and begin to see those in our daily lives who are lonely and need a friend. We can begin today by taking time to minister to someone and introduce him or her to Jesus.

Prayer

Lord, please help me to be willing to reach out to others so that the love of Jesus is seen in me. Help me to be a true minister for You seven days a week...

June 11

Keeping Promises

I will go into Your house with burnt offerings; I will pay You my vows, Which my lips have uttered And my mouth has spoken when I was in trouble.

—Psalm 66:13–14

It is easy to make promises to God when we are pushed into a corner. Have you ever said, "God, if you just get me out of this situation, I will do whatever You ask of me," and then forgotten to do what He asks when your crisis is over?

King David recognized how important it is to keep a vow made to the Lord during times of trouble. He was required to present sacrifices and burnt offerings, as well as pay his vows to God. Today, we are no longer required to perform the rituals of King David's era, but we are expected to keep the promises we have made.

If there is something you need to fulfill as a promise to God, do it today. He is a God of promise; let us, as His children, keep our promises to Him.

Prayer

Father God, it is easy to verbalize a commitment; it is often difficult to keep that commitment. Please help me to keep the promises that I have made to You…

June 12

With God's Help

Being confident of this very thing, that He who has begun a good work in you will complete it until the day of Jesus Christ.

—Philippians 1:6

"Okay, God; I give in." I prayed these words when devotion after devotion confirmed to me that it was time to resume my writing. The final confirmation came one morning when I picked up my Bible and continued reading where I had left off the day before: "*Thus speaks the Lord God of Israel, saying: 'Write in a book for yourself all the words that I have spoken to you.'*" (Jerimiah 30:2). Those words were my black and white from God to continue my writing.

As a grandmother in the second phase of my life, I am following my dream to become a published writer. With God's help, it will happen. What is your dream? God and you can make it a reality.

Prayer

Father God, thank You for making me a dreamer. With Your help, I can fulfill my dreams…

June 13

Perfect in God's Eyes

But Noah found grace in the eyes of the Lord. This is the genealogy of Noah. Noah was a just man, perfect in his generations. Noah walked with God.

—Genesis 6:8–9

God wanted Noah; God wants you! He wants you with a perfect heart. But what is a perfect heart? According to *Strong's Concordance*, the Hebrew word for perfect as used in the above verse is *tâmîyd*.[11] This word means "without blemish, complete, full, upright, whole." God wants you with a heart that is upright and whole, ready to be obedient to Him, just as Noah was when he built the ark without ever having seen rain. God wants an obedient heart filled with the quietness and peace of His Holy Spirit.

God is continually watching for those with hearts prepared to receive all that He has to offer; He is watching you. Are you ready with a perfect heart?

Prayer

Abba, Father, I want Your strength and power in my life every day. Please help me to prepare my heart so that it is perfect for You…

June 14

Elderly Advice

But he rejected the advice which the elders had given him, and consulted the young men who had grown up with him, who stood before him.

—2 Chronicles 10:8

When we are in trouble, it is easy to go to our peers and seek advice. We usually hear words that we want to hear from people our own age. But if we went to the older people—people who have lived and experienced life—we could save ourselves a lot of heartache.

King Rehoboam did not go to his elders for advice when he succeeded his father, King Solomon, to the throne. Instead, he took the advice of young men from his generation—advice that led to his having to flee the kingdom for his life.

God desires the older people in the church to teach and counsel those younger than themselves (Titus 2). But the advice they give is only useful when it falls on listening ears and hearts. Although some of us only learn from hard knocks and bruises, God does not want us to learn that way. He gave us examples in the Bible of people to imitate and learn from; He also gave us examples of people to not imitate.

Do not be like King Rehoboam. Find an older, godly person to become your advisor when you are making hard decisions; you will be blessed by the wise counsel of a mature believer.

Prayer

Lord, thank You for my mentors, who have been godly people. You have placed them around me to advise, direct, and pray for me during crucial times in my life…

_____

_____

_____

_____

_____

June 15

Just Do It

"Consider now, for the Lord has chosen you to build a house for the sanctuary; be strong, and do it."

—1 Chronicles 28:10

In the Bible study that I lead for mothers with young children, I have tried to impress on the moms that they were chosen by God to be the mothers of their little ones—He chooses to open or close the womb (1 Samuel 1). With such a high calling placed upon mothers to care for their babies, we need to be in God's Word daily and depend on His strength to meet the challenge.

As I read 1 Chronicles 28:10, I realized that this verse could apply to mothers. Our homes are to be sanctuaries for our children. We have been called by God to build our homes on the Solid Rock—Jesus Christ. It takes strength to be a stay-at-home mom in a society that is based on two-income families. But God has promised to not forsake mothers as they complete their work for Him (1 Chronicles 28:20). Take courage, moms; God is on your side—just do it!

Prayer

Precious Lord, thank You for all of the godly moms who sacrifice on a daily basis to be the earthly guardians of Your children. Bless them today as they work for You…

June 16

Get Busy!

For a dream comes through much activity, And a fool's voice is known by his many words.

—Ecclesiastes 5:3

Do you know anyone who is constantly telling you about what they are going to do but you never see any results? King Solomon tells us about their character in his writings. Someone can talk forever about the things they are going to do to become rich or famous, but until they actually get busy and take the action needed to get the job done, they will not be taken seriously by others.

Through the words of Solomon, God tells us that the difference between a dreamer and a fool is action. He wants us to get busy! Don't just talk about becoming a teacher, singer, writer, painter, scientist, architect, preacher, or politician—actively pursue your dream! Ask God to help you do the work that is necessary to reach the goal.

Prayer

Heavenly Father, You have given me a vision for my life. It is my desire to make that dream a reality through Your help…

_____
_____
_____
_____
_____
_____

June 17

No Retirement in God's Kingdom

Nothing is better for a man than that he should eat and drink, and that his soul should enjoy good in his labor. This also, I saw, was from the hand of God.

—Ecclesiastes 2:24

Wouldn't it be wonderful to be able to go through life possessing everything we need and want without ever having to work? God doesn't think so; in fact, He tells us that working is good for the soul. Yet it seems as if all we think about during our careers is the day when we can retire from work.

It is not in God's plan for us to stop working! In Genesis 3:19, Adam is told by God "In the sweat of your face you shall eat bread Till you return to the ground." I do not see a retirement date in that verse. I believe that it is God's plan for us to work for the Kingdom of God when we retire from our secular jobs.

If you are already retired, get back into the workforce and do something for God; it is never too late. Remember, Moses was eighty years old when he began his best work!

Prayer

Thank You, Lord, for the hands and feet You have given me to work for You. Let everything I do all the days of my life bring glory to Your name…

June 18

Do Not Grieve the Holy Spirit

And do not grieve the Holy Spirit of God, by whom you were sealed for the day of redemption.

—Ephesians 4:30

Do you think Christians realize how often we grieve the Holy Spirit with wrong actions or by not doing something we should do? If we did realize it, we would probably be more careful with our choices.

Did I grieve the Holy Spirit with that doughnut I ate yesterday, which violated my First Place Bible study and weight-loss covenant to eat healthy foods? Yes, I think I did. I let my study group down as well because I promised them I would keep my commitments.

We can grieve the Holy Spirit many times during our day if we are not careful to think before we act. Ask God to help you be aware of each thing you do today so that it is pleasing to Him.

Prayer

Lord, forgive me for the times I have acted foolishly and done things to grieve Your Spirit. I want to live a life that is pleasing to You…

June 19

God's Timing

Therefore you also be ready, for the Son of Man is coming at an hour you do not expect.

—Matthew 24:44

I must admit that I have selfishly asked the Lord to return soon and claim His own. I know that my disappointment and disillusionment in the state of the world's moral condition have overshadowed, in my mind, God's desire that no one should perish (2 Peter 3:9). He will give everyone a chance to accept or reject Him before His return; I must be patient. But in the meantime, I need to be ready at all times because no one knows the day or hour of His return.

Part of being ready at all times is remembering to witness to and pray for those who are doomed to a life in hell because they have not accepted God's salvation. Share the gospel today with someone you know who is not saved; Jesus may return at any time.

Prayer

Father God, forgive me for selfishly desiring entrance into my heavenly home on my terms. Please help me to pray daily and labor faithfully until the time You choose to return for Your people…

June 20

Turn to God

For you were like sheep going astray, but have now returned to the Shepherd and Overseer of your souls.

—1 Peter 2:25

When things are going wrong in our lives, the first thing most of us want to do is to put God on a shelf. We do not feel like doing the church thing; we do not feel like reading God's Word; we do not feel like praying; we do not feel like serving. We are like sheep going astray—wandering around lost and alone, wondering where God is.

God does not want us to run from Him; He wants us to run to Him! He understands our frustrations and our shortcomings. He knows when we feel lost and neglected. Those are the times when He wants to reveal the fullness of Himself to us: "casting all your care upon Him, for He cares for you" (1 Peter 5:7).

God will renew a right spirit in our hearts when we come to Him totally vulnerable and hurting. He will heal us and bring restoration when we run to Him. Our weeping in the night will turn to joy in the morning (Psalm 30:5).

Prayer

Precious Lord, please remind me to turn to You and not run when my life is shrouded in darkness and despair. Remind me that You are my Light in a darkened world…

_____

_____

_____

_____

_____

_____

June 21

Blessed by Mentoring

But as for you, speak the things which are proper for sound doctrine...the older women likewise...that they admonish the young women to love their husbands, to love their children, to be discreet, chaste, homemakers, good, obedient to their own husbands, that the word of God may not be blasphemed.

—Titus 2:1, 3–5

When I was first asked to lead an in-home Bible study for mothers with small children, I laughed. I was already babysitting my three young grandchildren, ages three months to three years. Now the pastor over women's ministries was asking me to take on new moms and their babies! My reply was basically "Thanks, but no thanks."

A year went by, and I was no longer watching my grandchildren. But Pastor Donna was persistent; there was still a need for a Bible study where young moms could keep their babies and small children with them. She felt strongly that I was the person to lead that study. Again I laughed, but this time I said I would pray about it.

Two years and three study books later, there are eight moms and ten small children (with two new babies on the way!) in our Hearts at Home ministry. Is this a lot of work? You bet! My reward? God's blessing on my obedience, mothers growing in the Lord, and babies hearing the Word of God.

Prayer

Father, how precious little ones are to You! Please give me a heart big enough to encompass each child that crosses my path...

June 22

Cash Well Spent

For He says: "In an acceptable time I have heard you, And in the day of salvation I have helped you." Behold, now is the accepted time; behold, now is the day of salvation.

—2 Corinthians 6:2

"Yesterday is a canceled check; tomorrow is a promissory note; today is the only cash you have so spend it wisely."[12] I remembered hearing this saying as I was listening to a minister on a Christian radio station. He was stressing how important it is to not ignore the nudging of the Holy Spirit when He is speaking to your heart.

If we are only guaranteed today, shouldn't we spend our "cash" well? The best investment for today is investing in eternity. If you have been ignoring the nudges of the Holy Spirit, take a moment to inventory your time. We are only a breath away from our eternal existence; spend your time well.

Prayer

Heavenly Father, thank You for giving Your Son on an old rugged cross so that I can spend eternity in heaven with You. Help me to live each day as if it is my last day on earth, so that it is cash well spent…

June 23

Growing Pains

For they indeed for a few days chastened us as seemed best to them, but He for our profit, that we may be partakers of His holiness.

—Hebrews 12:10

As a parent, it is hard to watch your grown children suffer. When they are struggling emotionally, physically, or financially, it is a parent's nature to want to take away the pain, kiss the boo-boo, and make it all better, even when they are adults. It is hard for parents to believe that helping their children could actually be hurting them.

God has lessons for all of us to learn, and sometimes we "caretakers" get in God's way. The pain and discomfort our children are experiencing could be from God, who desires us to grow through our trials. Do not jump in too quickly when you see your children going through rough times. Pray about the situation, ask God to show you what His will is, and wait for an answer. While you are waiting, you can be sure that God is working behind the scenes.

Prayer

Lord, You are ever watchful over Your creation. You know exactly what it will take to grow Your children spiritually. Please help me to go through these growing pains willingly, knowing that You are in control…

June 24

Holy Spirit Intervention

Likewise the Spirit also helps in our weaknesses. For we do not know what we should pray for as we ought, but the Spirit Himself makes intercession for us with groanings which cannot be uttered.

—Romans 8:26

It was 3:00 a.m. on a Sunday in May. My husband, Ken, woke me up as he dashed to the bathroom, thinking that his stomach was lurching because of food poisoning. As he began to throw up blood, he became cold and clammy and slid to the floor. After a few moments, I helped him into a sitting position. He leaned back in my arms, his whole body twitching. His eyes rolled up in his head as it lolled to the side. With eyes wide open, my husband stared into nothingness.

I looked up at the ceiling, knowing that this was a life or death situation. "God, this is in Your hands" was the only thing I could pray. The Holy Spirit intervened for me, pleading for all the things I couldn't begin to pray for. At that moment, my husband began to stir, and his eyes focused on me. I knew that God had heard the pleas of the Holy Spirit, and my husband survived that bleeding ulcer as an answer to prayer.

Prayer

Holy Spirit, I am thankful that You are always with me to hear my cries at any time of the day or night. I never have to worry about what to pray when I put my heart in Your hands...

June 25

Lifted Hands

Let us search out and examine our ways, And turn back to the Lord; Let us lift our hearts and hands To God in heaven.

—Lamentations 3:40–41

I did it. You probably did it. We accepted Christ as our Savior and then somewhere along the line decided that we could do things our own way—that we did not have to consult Christ about the "little" things in our lives. Wrong! If left unchecked, the little things in life can become huge stumbling blocks in our relationship with God. We need to get on our knees every day and ask God to help us live our lives according to His plan.

As you worship this week, lift your hands to your heavenly Father, thanking Him for being your All in All and knowing exactly what you need. Rest in Him, trusting that He will plan your life so that you can live fully for Christ.

Prayer

Lord, please help me to remember that You are my Creator. No one knows better than You do what is best for my life. Help me to willingly submit to the plans You have for me…

June 26

Friends

A man who has friends must himself be friendly, But there is a friend who sticks closer than a brother.

—Proverbs 18:24

A friend of mine had been home from the hospital for about a week when I went to visit her. She was recovering from surgery on her knee. Her biggest complaint during my visit was that hardly anyone came to see her or even bothered to call. Remembering how difficult it had been for me to develop a friendship with this lady, I prayed that God would help me find the right words to share with her. Proverbs 18:24 is the verse God gave to me: we must show ourselves friendly in order to make friends.

I gently reminded this friend how critical and demanding she could sometimes be. Acting like a spoiled child did not help to endear her to others. My friend said she was praying for God to help her change her attitude.

Do you need an attitude adjustment in the way you deal with the people in your life? God can help you become the kind of friend that is closer than a brother.

Prayer

Dear Jesus, thank You for the wonderful gift of friendship. May I always love and care for the important people in my life and remember to let them know how I feel about them. Friends are a true gift from You…

June 27

Not Good Enough

Even though I am untrained in speech, yet I am not in knowledge. But we have been thoroughly manifested among you in all things.

—2 Corinthians 11:6

Ever have one of those days when you just don't feel "good enough"? Today is my day. Chalk it up to hormones, not enough sleep, or a vitamin deficiency—whatever—I do not feel good enough to be a leader or mentor at the moment. Then I read Paul's words in 2 Corinthians 11:6 (and I paraphrase): I might not be a trained speaker, but I do have knowledge about some things. Paul, with all his trials and frustrations, did not lower or raise himself in esteem. He simply knew he had to do whatever it was God wanted him to do. His life meant nothing if he did not finish the race and complete the task the Lord Jesus had given him (Acts 20:24).

I must do for God daily what He has called me to do, allowing my frustrations and feelings of inferiority to fade away as I bask in His glory and rely on His strength. When I feel inferior, I can turn to God's Word and see myself as He sees me. Then I can share my knowledge with others.

Prayer

Heavenly Father, thank You for helping me to see myself as You see me. When I feel unworthy, You remind me that "I am fearfully and wonderfully made" (Psalm 139:14)…

June 28

Give Thanks Always

Giving thanks always for all things to God the Father in the name of our Lord Jesus Christ.

—Ephesians 5:20

I don't know about you, but sometimes I find it very difficult to praise God and give Him thanks when my life is in the "cesspool." But, as I read God's Word, I find that I do not have a choice about when to give thanks; God commands us to give thanks always for all things. I need to be thankful when the car battery dies, when the kids are sick, when the kitchen cupboard is not as full as I think it should be, or when any other circumstance interferes with the way a happy day should go. In *Streams in the Desert* we read "Facing obstacles should make us sing."[13] This kind of thankfulness is contrary to how we react as humans.

Although I have found it hard to sing and give thanks during the bad times, I have found that when I do a total peace comes into my life. God reminds me that in my weakness He is strong. The older I get, the easier it becomes to thank God for all things, even during adversity. Why? Because He has never failed me.

Prayer

Father God, I pray that as I let my life be a testimony of Your faithfulness in all things, others will see the value of singing praises to You regardless of the circumstances they are going through…

_____

_____

_____

_____

_____

_____

June 29

Not Forgotten

Remember these, O Jacob, And Israel, for you are My servant; I have formed you, you are My servant; O Israel, you will not be forgotten by Me!

—Isaiah 44:21

Have you ever known anyone who seemed to have it all, yet they were still miserable? As I write this, my son is in that place. When he was seventeen, he gave his heart to the Lord, but the things of the world soon enticed him. He is now thirty years old, has a beautiful home, a great job, a nice car, a boat, goes out to dinner frequently with his numerous friends—you name it. But he is absolutely miserable.

As believers, we belong to God. He will not forget that we gave our hearts to Him. When we wander away, He will keep drawing us back. Isaiah 44:22 continues, "I have blotted out, like a thick cloud, your transgressions, And like a cloud, your sins. Return to Me, for I have redeemed you." Only when a wandering heart returns to the Lord can peace fill that life.

Are you a wanderer who needs to return home? Ask the Lord to forgive you, and return to the One who created you. He is waiting with arms wide open. (Afterword: My son rededicated his life to the Lord in September 2006!)

Prayer

Father God, I come to You today with a broken heart. Please forgive me for the times I forget You and get wrapped up in the things of the world. Restore a right spirit in me…

June 30

A Faithful God

If we are faithless, He remains faithful; He cannot deny Himself.

—2 Timothy 2:13

Once the Holy Spirit enters your life, you are no longer your own. First Corinthians 6:19–20 says, "Or do you not know that your body is the temple of the Holy Spirit who is in you, whom you have from God, and you are not your own?"

At some point in our spiritual life each of us will falter in our walk. It is in those times of stumbling that we need to remind ourselves that God is faithful to His own. In Hebrews 13:5 we are told that God will never leave us or forsake us. Today's Scripture says God cannot deny or forsake His own, because He cannot deny Himself.

If you have faltered in your walk with the Lord, do not be discouraged. Ask Him for forgiveness. He will pick you up, dust you off, and place you back on the right path.

Prayer

Lord, there are times when I forget to remember the promises found in Your Word. Please remind me that I am Your child. I want to walk in righteousness with You…

July

July 1

The Lord Is My Hope

Blessed is the man who trusts in the Lord, And whose hope is the Lord.

—Jeremiah 17:7

As I was watching the news this week, it was hard not to become depressed: murders are committed everywhere, women and children are missing, there are bombings in Spain by terrorists, homosexuals have been given marriage licenses—you name it! God reminded me to keep my eyes fixed on Him and to place my hope and trust in Him. I am only a guest in this sinful world, and my permanent home is with the Father in heaven. When I get home, He will wash away my tears, and all crying, sorrow, death, and pain will be gone (Revelation 21:4). But while living in this world, it is my task to put on the full armor of God for protection (Ephesians 6:11), to share the gospel of salvation with as many as possible, and to wait patiently for my Lord's return.

It is a privilege to be a child of God, but with privileges come responsibilities. It is my responsibility to do all I can to reach others so they too will have hope—hope that will carry them through.

Prayer

Precious Father, please help me not to become fearful or doubtful as I walk the path You have placed before me. I want to place all of my trust and hope in You…

July 2

More Than Meat

"Life is more than food, and the body is more than clothing."
—Luke 12:23

In January 2003 I began a First Place Bible study, which challenges women (as well as men) to lose weight through scriptural discipline in every area of one's life. During that time, Luke 12:23 took on a whole new meaning for me; I began to really see myself as the temple of the Lord (1 Corinthians 6:19). It became a passion for me to be the best temple I could be. I began to see the importance of being balanced in every area of my life: physically, spiritually, emotionally, and mentally.

I desired a deeper knowledge of God's Word, so I made a vow to not watch television for the entire month of February. I kept that vow, and what a blessing! I was able to read not only the Bible but also other uplifting books, and I found that I did not miss the shows I once had to watch.

God is growing and maturing me into the woman He wants me to be. I still have a long way to go, but I know God will finish the work He began (Philippians 1:6). And I am thankful my life has become more than food!

Prayer

Heavenly Father, I thank You for the changes taking place in my life. You are my Bread of Life; may I feast only on You…

Buried Treasure

And you will seek Me and find Me, when you search for Me with all your heart.

—Jeremiah 29:13

When I was a child, I loved to hear stories about buried treasure. It takes time and research to track down buried treasure. For Christians, discovering the buried treasure God has for them does not require a secret map, special tools, a trip around the world, or calluses on our hands from digging. Our buried treasure is found in the Bible and is available to everyone who wants to search for it. Our eyes and our heart are the only tools we need.

The greatest treasure is Jesus Christ, who desires a personal relationship with you! If you are looking for this relationship, you must seek it; He has promised that when you seek Him you will find Him. If you know the Lord but want more of Him, dig deeper—the deeper you dig, the greater the treasure!

Prayer

Lord, I want more of You. As I dig deeper into Your Word, please show me Your treasures…

July 4

True Independence

For he who is called in the Lord while a slave is the Lord's freedman. Likewise he who is called while free is Christ's slave.

—1 Corinthians 7:22

Independence Day—a day to celebrate freedom—yet true freedom is beyond the concept of many people. Christ tells us that true freedom comes from knowing the living God. In our human nature, it is difficult to understand how a slave can be free. But it is only through committing our lives to God that we can be free from our sin nature and spiritual death, which is separation from God. When Jesus cried out, "My God, My God, why have You forsaken Me?" as He was hanging on the cross, He was experiencing separation from God for the first time (Matthew 27:46).

Accepting Jesus as our Savior has given us the chance to escape eternal separation from God, but it is a free choice. Have you experienced true freedom through Christ? If not, ask Him to forgive you of your sins right now and begin serving Him. Today can be your day of true independence.

Prayer

Heavenly Father, today I celebrate freedom in You. Thank You for allowing me to be Your servant…

July 5

Secrets of the Lord

The secret of the Lord is with those who fear Him, And He will show them His covenant.

—Psalm 25:14

I have always wanted to be special enough to someone that they would tell me things that no one else knew. Over the years, I have gained the respect of several good friends, who know they can trust me.

Have you ever wanted to know the secrets of the Lord? By showing reverence for God and His Word and by living a righteous life, we show God that we are trustworthy. He then can begin to trust us with His secrets. It takes time to gain that trust, as we often waiver in our walk. But our God is faithful to forgive and put us back on track. If you are not on track with God right now, ask Him to forgive you (1 John 1:9) and set you on a straight path (Luke 3:4).

Prayer

Heavenly Father, I want to know Your ways; I want to earn Your trust. Please forgive my disobedience and make my paths straight...

Fit to Run

Therefore we also, since we are surrounded by so great a cloud of witnesses, let us lay aside every weight, and the sin which so easily ensnares us, and let us run with endurance the race that is set before us.

—Hebrews 12:1

Being in a First Place Bible study has helped me understand that any weight, especially extra pounds, can hinder our ability to finish a race. Runners are sleek and fit. They literally put aside weight. It would be difficult to win a race if you were overweight. Runners eat the right foods, get plenty of exercise, and drink a lot of water. They do everything they can to be sure they are fit.

It is my goal to lose the extra pounds I have gained so that I can be a better athlete for the Lord as I run the race He has set before me. Is there something that is weighing you down and keeping you from finishing the race set before you? Ask God to show you the areas in your life that are weighing you down. Then use His Word, prayer, and discipline to get back into the race.

Prayer

Lord, I want to win the race that You have set before me. Let me lay aside anything that will keep me from reaching the finish line…

July 7

Darkness Exposed

"And this is the condemnation, that the light has come into the world, and men loved darkness rather than light, because their deeds were evil."

—John 3:19

I have lived to see Bible reading and prayer taken out of the public schools; now the Pledge of Allegiance is under attack because it contains the words "under God." How can a nation that has been so blessed by God want to totally remove Him from every public place?

John 3:19 states, "Men loved darkness rather than light, because their deeds were evil." Evil abounds all over the world: Abortion is ripping babies from the womb; homosexual couples are being issued marriage licenses; drugs are readily available to children; murders occur daily in our homes, schools, and streets. All of this sin is darkness! Jesus, who is "light," exposes the darkness in His Word; therefore, anything having to do with the Bible is being scorned or "turned off." Without the light shining to expose the sins of men, darkness again becomes comfortable.

Has your light become dim or been extinguished to hide the darkness in your life?

Prayer

Lord God, I ask You to forgive me for those things I do that bring darkness into my life. Please expose any dark area in me that needs Your light, so that I may be restored to You…

July 8

Ask God

"Ask, and it will be given to you; seek, and you will find; knock, and it will be opened to you."

—Matthew 7:7

Babysitting every day for my three grandchildren was a blessing, but I was beginning to wear down physically. I struggled with the idea of having them go to a day care center. These little ones were "flesh of my flesh," and I wanted them to be loved and nurtured. I prayed for months, asking God to give me a "black and white" answer as to what I should do.

In church one morning, my pastor told a story about a young man who placed letters over his bed that read "Let God," to remind him that God does the work through us in ministry. Pastor Ben demonstrated this story using a white screen on the sanctuary wall with black letters projected onto it. A little later in the story, the young man once again doubted God's hand in his ministry and went home frustrated. As he slammed the door to his bedroom, the d fell off the wall. I watched the screen, as the words "Let Go" were now visible. I could almost hear God whispering the words, "Carol, let go and trust me. I have something else for you to do." This was the answer to my prayer—my black and white!

I informed my children that after three months I would no longer be babysitting. Since then, my life has taken a wonderful turn that I never expected!

Prayer

Lord, You are faithful to answer when Your children ask specific questions. Let me always remember how faithful You have been to answer me when I sought You with my whole heart…

July 9

Drawing Close to God

Draw near to God and He will draw near to you.

—James 4:8

There is no magic formula for drawing close to God. He says, "Draw near to me and I will draw near to you." Becoming close to someone requires spending time with that person. By reading God's Word and praying daily, a relationship forms. You begin to know His voice (John 10:4) and recognize the nudging of His Spirit.

When Satan tries to seduce you with his lies, you can recognize them because you have filled your heart with truth. Jesus said, "I am the way, the truth, and the life" (John 14:6). Guard your heart against the lies of the world; draw close to God and He will be there to protect you and give you the strength you need.

Prayer

Dear Lord, You are as close to me as I want You to be. I pray that You will fill me with the desire to draw closer to You each day…

July 10

Wholly Follow God

"Surely not one of these men of this evil generation shall see that good land of which I swore to give to your fathers, except Caleb the son of Jephunneh; he shall see it, and to him and his children I am giving the land on which he walked, because he wholly followed the Lord."

—Deuteronomy 1:35–36

Sometimes God has to shake up our lives to get our attention, and our security is taken away for a season. This happened to my daughter and her family. In the past five years they have moved several times and eventually had to move in with her in-laws. The last home they lived in was a rental, which the whole family dearly loved. Nadja and her husband Dwayne had hoped to buy the home and were crushed when they had to move.

Through this season in their lives, the Lord has been able to work in my daughter and son-in-law in a way He could not have had they not been in this situation. As I see them growing closer to the Lord and to one another, my prayer has been that God will "give them the land they set their feet on" as they begin to wholeheartedly follow Him.

Prayer

Father, many times I am stubborn and need to get the wind knocked out of my sails to learn the lessons You have for me. Please help me to be a better listener and follower of Your directions…

July 11

Steps of Faith

"In your seed all the nations of the earth shall be blessed, because you have obeyed My voice."

—Genesis 22:18

Abraham was willing to sacrifice Isaac to the Lord. He did not ask questions; he merely obeyed and took his son to the designated spot and prepared for the sacrifice. Why was Abraham able to do this? He remembered God's promise that his seed would number more than the grains of sand or the stars in the sky. Abraham was confident that God would intervene, because Isaac was the son of promise God had given to him and Sarah. God would either provide a sacrifice or raise Isaac from the dead.

God wants each of us to have the faith of Abraham. He is standing back, waiting to bless your life. Hebrews 11:6 says: *"He rewards those who earnestly seek Him."* Take your step of faith today and do that one thing God is nudging you to do. He will bless your obedience.

Prayer

Lord, thank You for the little steps of faith I am taking in You. Help me to take bigger steps as I grow in You, so that I will be ready for that big leap that will someday be asked of me…

July 12

Genuine Repentance

"Now therefore, please pardon my sin, and return with me, that I may worship the Lord."

—1 Samuel 15:25

Sin hinders our worship. When Saul disobeyed God by not destroying all of the Amalekites and their belongings, fellowship was broken between God and Saul. Although Saul sought forgiveness through the priest, Samuel, his repentance wasn't genuine. Eventually, David, a man after God's own heart, replaced Saul as king.

God wants our true repentance when we seek forgiveness. It is only when we come to Him humbly and sincerely, seeking forgiveness, that our fellowship with God is restored.

Is there something standing in the way of your worship? As you enter the Lord's house this week, ask Him to forgive your sin and restore your relationship with Him, so that you may worship joyfully.

Prayer

Sunday is the day I come to worship You with fellow believers, Lord. May I come to You this week with a pure heart of repentance…

July 13

Our Gift of Truth

"The secret things belong to the Lord our God, but those things which are revealed belong to us and to our children forever, that we may do all the words of this law."

—Deuteronomy 29:29

God doesn't want His children to know everything. Surprised? If He had wanted us to know everything, He would have revealed all of His "secrets" in His Word. Deuteronomy tells us that there are secrets known only to God. He reveals what we need to know to successfully finish our journey here on earth. It is our responsibility to take what He has chosen to show us and apply those truths to our daily living.

God has revealed His nature so that we will know the unconditional love He has for His children. The Bible is to be a source of inspiration and encouragement. There will be things in the Bible that we will not completely understand until Christ's return. Don't be discouraged, friend. Use what you do understand—leave the rest to God to reveal in His own time.

Prayer

Lord, I don't need to understand everything in the Bible to know that You love me. Please help me to use the truth which has been revealed to me in Your Word to help me live a life pleasing to You…

July 14

Timely Words

"But when they deliver you up, do not worry about how or what you should speak. For it will be given to you in that hour what you should speak."

—Matthew 10:19

Things are changing in America! A story on the evening news caught my attention: Michael A. Newdow, a forty-nine year old father, claimed he was protecting his daughter's freedom when he filed a lawsuit to have under God removed from the Pledge of Allegiance. As of this writing, a decision in the courts has been made against Mr. Newdow, and under God remains in the pledge. That decision will probably be appealed.

Like it or not, the time is coming when Christians will be asked to defend their faith. Will we as believers have the courage to stand firm? In *The Hiding Place*, Corrie ten Boom didn't know if she would have the strength to defend her faith if she and her family were caught hiding Jewish families from the Nazis during World War II. Her father told her that one does not buy a train ticket until the train is ready to leave.[14] To me this statement means "Don't borrow trouble until it knocks at your door."

Jesus tells us in Matthew 10 to not worry about our words when we are put to the test; the Holy Spirit will give us the right words. It is up to each believer to cultivate a relationship with God, so that we will hear those words whispered in our time of need.

Prayer

Precious Lord, I want to be able to hear Your voice through Your Holy Spirit when I need it. Help me to draw close enough to You to recognize You when You talk to me…

July 15

Profitable Godliness

For bodily exercise profits a little, but godliness is profitable for all things, having promise of the life that now is and of that which is to come.

—1 Timothy 4:8

It seems as if everyone I talk to is going to the gym, jogging, working out with DVDs or videos, and dieting. Many of us want to get in shape and be healthier. Is this wrong? No, because God wants us to take care of our bodies—we need them to carry out His work through us. But how many of those same people are giving the same amount of time to things that make us more Christlike? We can be the most fit and healthy people alive, but if we neglect the disciplines that take care of our spiritual selves, what will it profit us?

Take a few moments to reflect on your daily activities; are you coming up short on the eternal side? Ask God to bring balance into your life right now.

Prayer

Heavenly Father, please help me focus on the things that will count for eternity. Let me not become obsessed with the temporal things in life…

July 16

Fables

For the time will come when they will not endure sound doctrine, but according to their own desires, because they have itching ears, they will heap up for themselves teachers; and they will turn their ears away from the truth, and be turned aside to fables.

—2 Timothy 4:3–4

How easy it is to listen to words that we want to hear! But God often gives us words that we don't want to hear. As a result, the church has been caught up in the "change the words to suit what I want" syndrome, resulting in heresy in the Church. Homosexuals are readily accepted in some churches and ordained as ministers; adultery is an accepted way of life; divorce affects the church as much as it does secular society; we are like the world!

Some people do not want to hear that they need to conform to God's moral law, so they look for teachers who twist the Word until it fits their lifestyle. It will not go well for those who twist the truth. They will have to answer to God as to why they allowed themselves to be swayed by fables: "myths or tales," as defined in *Strong's Concordance*.[15]

What kind of stories have you been listening to?

Prayer

Father, I will have to answer to You for the truths I have allowed to become fables in my life. Please forgive me, and help me to listen only to Your truth…

July 17

Showers of Blessing

But He said, "More than that, blessed are those who hear the word of God and keep it!"

—Luke 11:28

It is easy to sit in a church pew, listen to the pastor as he or she reads God's Word, nod our heads in agreement, and walk out the door without remembering what the sermon was about. Our ears were hearing but not listening. Jesus, the greatest teacher, told His listeners to really hear God's Word—hear it and keep it.

When a woman in the crowd told Jesus that His mother was blessed (Luke 11:27), His response was that those who kept God's Word were the blessed ones. What an awesome thought! How blessed do you want to be? As you go to your place of worship this week, tune your ears in to hear and then obey the Word of God.

Prayer

Showers of blessing, Lord! Besides You, I want those more than anything. Please open my ears and help me to hear Your Word and then obey…

July 18

No Copouts

But he said, "O my Lord, please send by the hand of whomever else You may send."

—Exodus 4:13

Point the finger at the other person. I do it. You do it. Let someone else sing in the choir, drive the Sunday school bus, change diapers in the nursery, teach Sunday school, or help with crafts during Vacation Bible School. They are so much better at it than I am—or so we think.

God did not let Moses get away with that cop-out; he sent Aaron, Moses' brother, to help Moses. God knew Aaron could speak well. He gave Moses the words to speak to Aaron and Aaron spoke to the people (Exodus 4:14-16).

Is God speaking to you? If so, step out in obedience to do what He has planned for you. He will send the people you need to stand beside you as you accomplish wonderful things for His Kingdom.

Prayer

Lord, I sometimes forget that with You I can do all things. Please show me what You want me to do and send me an Aaron to stand by my side…

July 19

The Best Things

And this I pray, that your love may abound still more and more in knowledge and all discernment, that you may approve the things that are excellent, that you may be sincere and without offense till the day of Christ.

—Philippians 1:9–10

I enjoy reading the New King James Version of the Bible because I am a poet at heart and love the way the verses flow. But sometimes a verse can be easier to understand when read in a different version. The New International Version of today's Scripture says "that you may be able to discern what is best and may be pure and blameless until the day of Christ." I think this verse applies not only to the knowledge that we gain to help us make correct decisions but also to the choices we make in serving the Lord.

Those of us with servants' hearts want to do everything. Since we cannot do that, due to limited time, we must pray and ask God to tell us what the best things are. He has a purpose for every believer—something He designed for that one person. We must earnestly seek His guidance if we are to avoid burnout.

Instead of doing many things haphazardly, ask God to reveal to you the things that you can do well—your best things.

Prayer

Heavenly Father, I want whatever I do as Your servant to be the very best I can do. Please help me not to settle for second best when it comes to the work of Your Kingdom…

Because of Love

Therefore the law was our tutor to bring us to Christ, that we might be justified by faith. But after faith has come, we are no longer under a tutor.

—Galatians 3:24–25

I once heard this Scripture used in a sermon in a way I had never heard before. The pastor said that since Christ came we are no longer under the old law; the old law was the tutor that brought us to Christ. We are now justified by faith (Romans 5:1) and we no longer need the tutor of the law!

Jesus wants us to obey His commandments because we love Him—not because we have to—and because His law enables us to live a healthy, productive, and abundant life. Take time today to thank God for sending Jesus to free you from the old law.

Prayer

Father God, I am so thankful for the freedom I have in Your Son. May I never use this freedom wrongly or take advantage of it...

July 21

Sustained by God

I lay down and slept; I awoke, for the Lord sustained me.

—Psalm 3:5

My husband, Ken, had several heart attacks in November of 2003. Blood tests revealed there was heart damage, but how much would not be known until further tests were done. When Ken had been hospitalized previously, I stayed overnight with him. But this time I knew I had to go home and rest. I didn't know how long he would be in the hospital or if he would need open-heart surgery.

I thought it would be hard to sleep, but each evening after returning home I spent time worshipping and praising God, giving everything to Him, before I closed my eyes. Each night the Lord sustained me; I slept and woke refreshed to face another day. Thank God, Ken didn't need the heart surgery, and he is doing well as of this writing.

If there is something stressful going on in your life, give it to God. He will freshen, strengthen, and sustain you through every crisis.

Prayer

You have always been there for me, Lord. I cannot think of a time when You failed to comfort and strengthen me when I called on Your name. Thank You for Your sustaining power…

July 22

Rainbow Reminders

"I set My rainbow in the cloud, and it shall be for the sign of the covenant between Me and the earth."

—Genesis 9:13

As I was leaving a parking lot last week after grocery shopping, I saw a vivid rainbow. The sky in front of me was so gray it was almost black. Behind me rays of sunshine broke through the clouds, illuminating the darkness. It was the perfect canvas for the beautiful rainbow that appeared. I pointed it out to my husband and then noticed a fainter rainbow above it—a double portion of God's promise!

When I see a rainbow, I never fail to remember God's promise to Noah to never again destroy the whole earth with water (Genesis 9:15). It also reminds me that if God gives a promise—any promise—He is faithful to keep it. Have you been given a promise from God but think He has forgotten to fulfill it? Ask Him to send you a rainbow—a reminder that He never forgets.

Prayer

Lord, You have given me so many beautiful rainbows in my life. When I forget to remember, please send me a rainbow of love straight from Your heart as a reminder that You never forget a promise…

July 23

Complete Trust

I will say of the Lord, "He is my refuge and my fortress; My God, in Him I will trust."

—Psalm 91:2

My friend's husband just underwent brain surgery. It was totally unexpected. One night he had a seizure; the following day, tests revealed he had a tumor. He is a young man with two small daughters. Was he afraid? Most definitely! Does he have hope? Most definitely! He knows the God of hope and a future (Jeremiah 29:11). Does my friend's husband have cancer? I don't know yet. I do know that whatever the prognosis, they have chosen to trust in the Lord with all their hearts, even when it is beyond their understanding (Proverbs 3:5).

No matter what you are going through in life, God wants to be your refuge, your strength, and your fortress. He wants you to have total trust in Him, even when you can't see the big picture.

Prayer

Lord, I know there will be times in life when I will face things I do not understand. I pray I will grow to know You so well that I will always trust You and run to You for shelter…

July 24

A Jealous God

"For you shall worship no other god, for the Lord, whose name is Jealous, is a jealous God."

—Exodus 34:14

Have you ever missed church because you wanted to see the big game, the weather was perfect for going to the lake, or maybe you just wanted to sleep in? I don't mean those times when you are on vacation; I mean those times when you miss church several Sundays in a row! Did it ever occur to you that maybe those things are gods that slowly are replacing the one and only true God and that He is jealous of your other gods?

Sunday is the day of the week that we worship with other believers, not because we have to, but because we want to share the experience of worshipping our Lord and Savior with those who know the joy of His salvation. We also need the encouragement of other Christians when life throws us unexpected curves.

Satan loves to see us back away from regular church attendance; he loves to get a foot in the door (1 Peter 5:8). If you give Satan an inch, he will take a mile! Begin today to get rid of your idols and allow God to have first place in your life.

Prayer

Heavenly Father, please forgive me for the times I allow the things of life to become more important to me than my relationship with You…

July 25

A Blameless Heart

I will behave wisely in a perfect way. Oh, when will You come to me? I will walk within my house with a perfect heart.

—Psalm 101:2

Lord, please forgive me. I cannot say I always walk in my own home with a perfect or blameless heart. How many times when I've been angry have I used language I shouldn't have used? How many times have I spoken words to my children or grandchildren that hurt instead of encouraged? How many times has my husband shouldered the brunt of my frustration when circumstances weren't going the way I wanted them to? Were my conversations with friends without gossip or malice?

It is easy to be nice when the world's eyes are watching. But to live blamelessly in our own homes when no one else is looking is a real test of how much we have actually allowed Christ to be the Lord of our lives. Our actions, whether at home or in public, should always reflect a perfect and blameless heart; this is only possible through the love and strength of Jesus Christ.

Prayer

Lord, I desire to walk blamelessly before You. It is only through Your strength and salvation that I can do so. Thank You for being that strength for me…

July 26

Thorns and Thistles

Then the Lord God took the man and put him in the garden of Eden to tend and keep it.

—Genesis 2:15

As I was working in my yard one morning, pulling weeds that had long been neglected, I began to imagine the perfect garden: the Garden of Eden. Adam and Eve were able to enjoy all the beauty and wonder of God's creation without the weeds and thorns! Because sin entered that first garden, I must now tend gardens that are full of weeds and thorns. Genesis 3:18 says, "Both thorns and thistles it shall bring forth for you."

When neglected, my gardens are not pretty and are hard to enjoy, because weeds take over and choke out the flowers and fruit. Order becomes chaos. The garden of my heart and mind works the same way. If I do not daily pull up and trim away the weeds and thorns of sin in my life, they begin to overtake me, and I am no longer attractive to those around me. Fortunately, I have a Master Gardener who is anxiously waiting for me to ask to be pruned, trimmed, and groomed into a beautiful garden once again. Do you need to be pruned?

Prayer

Thank You, heavenly Father, for those times when You lovingly trim and prune away the sin in my life. I desire to be the most beautiful garden I can be for You, bearing much fruit...

July 27

Peaceful Living

If it is possible, as much as depends on you, live peaceably with all men.

—Romans 12:18

I was home alone one evening when a friend called me. She was heartbroken. She had argued with someone several weeks before. It seemed as if this person did not want to mend fences; she uttered a flat "No" when my friend sought reconciliation. So what do we do when someone doesn't want to meet us halfway? Go to the Bible and see how God wants us to respond.

God gives the answer in Romans 12. You are only responsible for your part: "as much as depends on you." Doing our part and seeking forgiveness and reconciliation are all that we are required to do. The responsibility then lies on the other person's shoulders. God must be allowed to take control and speak to the other party's heart. Once you have done your part, you must go forward. Let God do the rest.

Prayer

Lord, many times I want to speed up Your timetable. Remind me to wait for You to do the work that is sometimes needed to bring about forgiveness and reconciliation…

July 28

Power to the Weak

He gives power to the weak, And to those who have no might He increases strength.

—Isaiah 40:29

It was a late Wednesday evening. My day had been long and filled with activity. All I wanted to do was go to bed, but I hadn't finished my Bible study for my Thursday night class. I really struggled: do I finish the study or fall into bed for some much needed sleep? My desire to go to class prepared won out over my exhaustion. Sighing deeply, I picked up my Bible lying on the kitchen table and opened it to the book of Isaiah. On the two pages facing me, only one verse was highlighted: "He gives power to the weak." I read the verse again and laughed out loud. Through His Word, God was gently reminding me that He would give me the strength I needed to finish my study that night and to complete any other task He calls me to do.

Prayer

Lord, I am so glad You are my strength when my body is crying out "Quit!" I know You will always be there to help me carry my burdens and complete my service for You…

July 29

Joy in the Morning

For His anger is but for a moment, His favor is for life; Weeping may endure for a night, But joy comes in the morning.

—Psalm 30:5

Have you ever noticed how everything seems to get worse at night? The sick baby's fever goes up in the evening. The sore throat that was bearable during the waking hours is excruciatingly painful when it is time for bed. There isn't enough money coming in to pay the bills, and you toss and turn all night wondering how to make ends meet. You lose a loved one, and the loneliness smothers you during the dark, quiet hours. You and your spouse have an argument about something the kids did, and you go to bed angry. The heaviness of life's problems becomes unbearable as the dark settles in around you. You feel crushed under the weight of your troubles! Then God's Word brings relief.

God tells us that no matter what comes into our lives and tries to crush us, it is only temporary. He knew that life would get us down, and He gave us His Word as our life preserver. Hold tightly to God's promise when the night surrounds you. Your tears will dry when the morning dawns.

Prayer

Precious Savior, thank You for the promise that my tears will dry and my sorrow will turn to joy when morning comes…

July 30

Loving Discipline

"As many as I love, I rebuke and chasten. Therefore be zealous and repent."
—Revelation 3:19

I do not like to be disciplined. Even as a child, I learned early not to buck authority because I did not like to pay the consequences.

Several years ago I did a study by Beth Moore entitled *Breaking Free*. I recently repeated this class, using a new workbook to fill in my responses. After the class was completed, I wanted to go back and compare some of my personal answers. During the first study, one of my prayers was "Lord, I don't want to be disciplined." My prayer in this same section during the second study was "Lord, thank You for disciplining me." Wow! During those four years between the studies, I had grown spiritually in the Lord. I had learned that God rebuking and chastening me came from love and had caused me to become more Christlike. I am His child, and He loves me enough to spank me when I run onto a dangerous road.

Are you being disciplined? Thank your heavenly Father for loving you enough to guide you back to the right path.

Prayer

Precious Father, thank You for making me Your child and showing me Your love by the discipline You bring into my life. It is meant to make me stronger and become more Christlike...

Few Workers

Then He said to them, "The harvest truly is great, but the laborers are few; therefore pray the Lord of the harvest to send out laborers into His harvest."

—Luke 10:2

I recently went to an event at my church that was a fellowship and informational time for women. At this "Mug and Muffin" breakfast, each ministry leader provided literature and gave a talk about her specific ministry. The ladies attending enjoyed muffins and other refreshments while they listened to the ministry leaders. Afterwards, they were given the opportunity to sign up for a ministry. Out of over two hundred women who were contacted about this event, only about forty-five attended. Why? God's Word tells us that the laborers would be few.

It is my desire that God would speak to the hearts of those women who didn't attend. Many may have had a good reason to be absent; many just do not want to commit to the Lord's work. Time is getting short—the Lord will return soon. Are you willing to commit whatever you do to the Lord and become a worker for Him?

Prayer

Thank You, Lord, for my servant's heart. I know it is a gift from You. May I never be hesitant to do the things You call me to do…

_____

_____

_____

_____

_____

_____

August

August 1

Mistakes and All

"But as for you, you meant evil against me; but God meant it for good, in order to bring it about as it is this day, to save many people alive."

—Genesis 50:20

As I was doing my Bible study one morning, one of the assignments was to "Give thanks to God for something you have never given Him thanks for before." Wow! I asked God to help me be honest with my answer. After a while, I began to pray, "Lord, thank you for my pregnancy when I was nineteen years old."

I grew up in the church and knew all about abstinence. When I submitted to temptation and became pregnant before marriage, I knew Satan was gloating that I had fallen, and my testimony had probably been ruined. But God, in His loving and merciful way, turned that mistake into good, as He did in the book of Genesis when Joseph's brothers sold him to the Ishmaelites.

I married Ken, the father of my baby, and came to California. Would I have eventually come to California under different circumstances? I can't say for sure, but I don't think so. God had already given me that opportunity four other times when Ken had asked me to marry him. Am I serving exactly where God wanted me to be? I believe so, with all my heart—mistakes and all!

Prayer

Precious Lord, thank You for allowing my mistakes to mold me into the woman You want me to be and for not allowing them to destroy my life…

_____
_____
_____
_____
_____
_____
_____

August 2

Famous and Special

And He has made from one blood every nation of men to dwell on all the face of the earth, and has determined their preappointed times and the boundaries of their dwellings.

—Acts 17:26

As a child growing up in Elmer, New Jersey, I never dreamed of living in "sunny California." In my mind it was a place where famous and special people lived! I certainly was not famous, and I didn't feel special. But circumstances in my life resulted in my moving to California in 1970.

The first few years in California were not easy, but God was faithful even when I was not. Today I can see God's plan: Ken and I are serving God in our own way; my children and grandchildren are close by; we have an extended church family that is a blessing; I am involved in ministries that are growing me in the Lord; I am touching other lives for Christ.

My life is more than I ever dreamed it could be. In the process, I discovered that I am one of the famous and special people—famous and special because I serve the Lord Jesus in exactly the place He wants me to be.

Prayer

Lord, thank You for making me a special person in You and for choosing to place me in California to do the work You have called me to. You are an awesome God…

_____

_____

_____

_____

_____

_____

_____

August 3

Healed by God

Come, and let us return to the Lord; For He has torn, but He will heal us; He has stricken, but He will bind us up.

—Hosea 6:1

Oh, how much like the Israelites we are! We stubbornly turn our backs on our Precious Lord, chase after the gods of this world, and then complain when uncomfortable things happen to us. God allows these things to happen and uses them to discipline us. When the fire gets hot enough to make us squirm, we cry "uncle" and then turn to God for forgiveness, wanting Him to put the pieces back together again, bind up the wounds of our heart, and heal us.

God is so merciful! He goes through this forgiving and healing process over and over for His stubborn children, even though we don't deserve it. Take time to thank your heavenly Father for the grace and mercy He has bestowed on you.

Prayer

Lord, I do not deserve the gift of salvation; thank You for forgiving my sins and for loving me even when I am unlovable…

August 4

No Truth in the Land

Hear the word of the Lord, You children of Israel, For the Lord brings a charge against the inhabitants of the land: "There is no truth or mercy Or knowledge of God in the land. By swearing and lying, Killing and stealing and committing adultery, They break all restraint, With bloodshed upon bloodshed."

—Hosea 4:1–2

While reading in the book of Hosea one morning, I felt led to substitute "you children of America" for "you children of Israel." As I read about Israel's unfaithfulness—the cursing, lying, murdering, stealing, and adultery—I thought, "This is America!" Little did I dream that in my lifetime I would see abortion legalized, under God in the Pledge of Allegiance attacked, praying in Jesus' name forbidden in public meetings, and the Ten Commandments removed from the public arena.

We are living in a time of unfaithfulness and desperately need the Lord. We are living in a time when we need to humble ourselves before the Lord and pray (2 Chronicles 7:14). We are living in a time when change begins with the Church.

Prayer

Lord, please forgive me for the times when I could have been praying for my country and didn't. We need You now more than ever. Remind me to lift this country and its leaders before You daily and to remember that change begins with me…

August 5

Where Is Your Faith?

But He said to them, "Why are you so fearful? How is it that you have no faith?"

—Mark 4:40

Whether your child is three or thirty-one, a mother cannot stop the concern that comes when her child is injured.

I was in the worry mode one morning at work as a result of my son tearing a pectoral muscle and not getting the medical attention I thought he needed. Although I knew he was in God's hands, I was still fretting as I asked my coworkers to pray for Jimmy and me. Not being able to concentrate, I left work early. To relax, I began to read *Ordering Your Private World* by Gordon MacDonald. I got to a phrase in the second chapter and stopped: "Where is your faith?"[16]

God reminded me of a story in the fourth chapter of Mark. A storm was raging, the disciples in the boat were fearful, and when they woke Jesus because of their fear, He said, "How is it that you have no faith?" At that moment, I realized I do have faith; my faith is in Jesus Christ, and it is my desire to let that faith be exhibited daily in my life—no matter how many storms come my way.

Prayer

Lord, thank You for the peace You bring into the storms of my life. When my eyes are focused on You, I can rise above them…

August 6

Better Is One Day

Blessed are those who dwell in Your house; They will still be praising You. Selah.

—Psalm 84:4

For the year 2004, my church's women's retreat theme was The Power of Love. I sang on the worship team that year. One of the songs kept playing in my mind: "Better is one day in your courts, …" (written by Matt Redman). Not only is it better to be in God's house, but according to today's verse, we will also be blessed! I don't know about you, but I need all the blessings I can get!

As you go into your place of worship this week, thank God for the blessings He has given to you. Allow the praises that fill you in God's house to go with you all week and be a part of all you do.

Prayer

Precious Lord, Your dwelling place is truly lovely. Please fill me with Your love so that I may share it with others…

August 7

Always Victorious

Then the Lord said to Gideon, "By the three hundred men who lapped I will save you, and deliver the Midianites into your hand."

—Judges 7:7

Recently, my church had a campaign called Celebration of Worship. Our goal was for two hundred fifty people to participate in this 40 Days of Focus, which was a study for home groups covering all aspects of worship. Only half that many people showed up to be assigned to a home group. This smaller number of people participating than was expected was a disappointment to the campaign director, who is also my friend. God gave me the following to encourage Roberta.

In Judges, chapter 7, Gideon was going to take an army of 22,000 to defeat the Midianites in battle. God wanted Gideon to know that He was bringing the victory, not the people. He had Gideon whittle his army down to the three hundred men who lapped water with their tongues like dogs do, drinking water from their hands at the water's edge. With those three hundred men, God brought victory.

When God is in control, the army may be small, but it will always be victorious. Regarding our campaign, the people who showed up to be in a home group were the army God chose to get the job done.

Prayer

Thank You, Father, for those faithful warriors You have chosen for the battle. They will be victorious...

August 8

Whoever Calls...

And it shall come to pass That whoever calls on the name of the Lord Shall be saved.

—Joel 2:32

It is easy to forget that the Lord loves everyone—even those we find unlovable. I have a family in mind as I write this. They are crude in their mannerisms, use language that makes me cringe, have been bullies for three generations, and are not liked by many in the neighborhood. But as I read the book of Joel, one phrase stood out: "Whoever calls on the name of the Lord." That includes those who are undesirable in our eyes. Instead of being judgmental, we need to pray for people such as these. It is our responsibility to let them experience the love of Jesus through us, even when we may want to turn away or ignore them.

It isn't always easy to obey God's Word, but He has told us to "take up the cross, and follow Me" (Mark 10:21). Sometimes that cross can be undesirable people placed in our life.

Ask the Lord to bring to your mind those people who need to call upon His name. Then ask Him to give you the love and compassion needed to be a light in the midst of their darkness and a life preserver in a sea that is raging around them.

Prayer

Precious Lord, thank You for the gift of salvation. Please help me to remember to share that gift, even with those who may seem unlovable…

August 9

Not An Easy Task

And I set my heart to seek and search out by wisdom concerning all that is done under heaven; this burdensome task God has given to the sons of man, by which they may be exercised.

—Ecclesiastes 1:13

In His Word, God tells us that we will not have it easy in this sinful world. King Solomon, with all of his wisdom and knowledge, recognized that trying to live a righteous life could be a burden. All of the evils and temptations facing us in the twenty-first century are the same ones that Solomon dealt with: "And there is nothing new under the sun" (Ecclesiastes 1:9). But thanks to the wonderful gift given to us—the gift of salvation—we have a Helper to come alongside us: "And I will pray the Father, and He will give you another Helper, that He may abide with you forever" (John 14:16).

The Holy Spirit will help us overcome the temptations that come our way. We need only call on the name of the Lord.

Prayer

Heavenly Father, thank You for the comfort of your Holy Spirit who dwells within me. He will help me with the hard things in life…

_____
_____
_____
_____
_____
_____

August 10

A Gentle Nudge

Be merciful to me, O God, be merciful to me! For my soul trusts in You; And in the shadow of Your wings I will make my refuge, Until these calamities have passed by.

—Psalm 57:1

You have nowhere to turn. The decisions that need to be made are overwhelming and affect many people. You are being tugged this way and that—back and forth. What do you do?

I was recently in such a place. As I sat down at my kitchen table, trying to make a decision, the chorus of an old hymn came to mind: "Where Could I Go But to the Lord?" (words and music by J. B. Coats). It was a gentle nudge from the Holy Spirit reminding me I am to come to Him. He is my refuge—a place of comfort, strength and peace—when I am faced with difficult decisions.

Prayer

Lord, I am safe under Your wings. Please remind me to run to You when faced with difficult decisions. The advice You give will always be right...

August 11

The Key to Victory

Let us hold fast the confession of our hope without wavering, for He who promised is faithful.

—Hebrews 10:23

We all experience it sometime in our lives: the desire to just throw in the towel and walk away from whatever it is we are wrestling with. God, however, has a different plan. He wants us to hold on to Him tightly and remember the promises He has given in His Word. He wants us to go forward with our struggles, using the guidance of the Word to light our paths (Psalm 119:105). He wants us to not waiver—to not give up. His plan is that we finish the race we have begun, regardless of what comes our way.

When we feel we cannot run another step, God wants us to remember that He will never leave us or forsake us (Hebrews 13:5); His feet will be right in step with ours as we cross the finish line into eternity. Praise God, for we are winners through Him!

Prayer

Hallelujah, Lord! I can find victory in You, regardless of what circumstances come into my life. Help me to hold tight to all of Your promises, for they are the key to victory…

August 12

God's Silence

"They shall wander from sea to sea, And from north to east; They shall run to and fro, seeking the word of the lord, But shall not find it."

—Amos 8:12

I have been raised on God's Word since the age of five. I have memorized it and have found comfort in it. I have certainly been disciplined by it! Decisions are made in my life based on its wise counsel. I cannot imagine my life without hearing from God.

As I was reading the book of Amos, the above verse seemed to leap off the page. Israel, due to disobedience, was going to be cut off from the comfort of God's Word. They would search for it frantically, but it would not be found.

How many times have we been disobedient and felt cut off from God's voice and gentle instruction? Though those times may be brief in duration, they are certainly unpleasant. How comforting it is to know that when life's problems become unbearable or when we need instruction, we can sit quietly at the feet of Jesus, read His Word, hear His voice, and find solace. He will always be there when we call.

Prayer

Precious Lord, thank You for opening Your arms to enfold me when I need help. I never have to run around trying to find You, because I know You are near. Please keep me close to Your heart so that I may hear Your voice…

_____
_____
_____
_____
_____
_____
_____

August 13

Satan's Tactics

For they all were trying to make us afraid, saying, "Their hands will be weakened in the work, and it will not be done." Now therefore, O God, strengthen my hands.

—Nehemiah 6:9

You know how it feels: The weight of the world is on your shoulders; you don't know if you can walk another step or do another task. This feeling is a scare tactic from Satan; he tries to throw stumbling blocks in your path, just as he tried to discourage Nehemiah and the Israelites from rebuilding the walls of Jerusalem. Nehemiah knew the taunts of the enemies were only to distract him from the work the Lord had called him to do.

Praise God—He is there to encourage and lift you up when others say the job is too hard or can't be done! Recognize the scare tactics of the enemy, and ask God to help you complete the task at hand. Revelation 2:10 tells us to "Be faithful until death, and I will give you the crown of life." What a day that will be! Hang in there, my friend; the best is yet to come!

Prayer

The crown of life—oh, how I want that, Lord! I ask You to strengthen my hands to complete the work You have called me to do…

August 14

Justice for All

When the wicked spring up like grass, And when all the workers of iniquity flourish, It is that they may be destroyed for ever.

—Psalm 92:7

Senseless violence. We see it every day on our streets, watch it on television, read about it in the papers, or experience it personally.

One evening recently, a friend's son, who is a dedicated servant of the Lord, was delivering pizza. While he was making the delivery, he was attacked by three thugs—three misguided boys who wanted something they didn't have and weren't willing to work for. God clearly states that although evildoers seem to be flourishing, they will be destroyed. The time will come when those thugs will have to answer to God; it is from Him that man gets justice (Psalm 89:14).

Fortunately, my friend's son was not severely injured and was able to rest in God's promise.

Prayer

Thank You, Lord, for the promises You give us. When life seems unfair, turning to Your Word gives us peace…

August 15

Forever Changed

Also I heard the voice of the Lord, saying: "Whom shall I send, And who will go for Us?" Then said I, "Here am I! Send me."

—Isaiah 6:8

When God comes into your life and physically fills you with His presence, you never forget it. I had such an experience at a women's retreat in 2004. Before that retreat, a friend prayed that I would experience God in a brand new way. I did. As I was praying for healing for someone, the Holy Spirit flowed through me in a way I had never felt before. At that moment, my experiences of the past thirty-five years came into focus and everything in my life made sense. I could finally say, without reservation, "Here I am, Lord; send me to do whatever you have called me to do."

That moment changed my life forever. If you have not experienced a life-changing moment, ask God to fill you with His Spirit. You will never be the same.

Prayer

Lord, thank You for bringing me to a higher level on my spiritual journey. Where would I be without You? I am ready to answer the call, wherever it may lead…

August 16

Spirit and Truth

"God is Spirit, and those who worship Him must worship in spirit and truth."
—John 4:24

Oh, to be a true worshiper of our Lord and Savior! To be the one He is looking for! I can only imagine what it will be like to be in the presence of Christ—to fall on my knees and hopefully hear Him say, "Well done, good and faithful servant" (Matthew 25:23). I want to be one who worships with my whole being—one who worships in spirit and truth.

I thank God that He has brought truth into my life and has set me free from sin. Oh, I will stumble and fall, but I know Jesus will pick me up, accept my plea for forgiveness, and restore me to fellowship.

Are you worshipping your Lord in spirit and truth? He is waiting with open arms to welcome you home, dear child of God.

Prayer

Precious Lord, thank You for being the same yesterday, today and forever (Hebrews 13:8). What You say will never change, and I want to worship You in spirit and truth...

August 17

Not Politically Correct

Thus says the Lord: "Do not learn the way of the Gentiles; Do not be dismayed at the signs of heaven, For the Gentiles are dismayed at them."

—Jeremiah 10:2

Follow the crowd. Stay in the flow. Be politically correct. We hear it; we see it; we do it. But not all of the things we learn from and expect from society are correct. God told the Israelites not to learn evil and corrupt practices from the Gentile nations.

We are not to learn the evil ways practiced in our world. Do not say abortion is legal. Do not condone gay marriages. Do not tolerate taking God out of the Pledge of Allegiance or the removing of the Ten Commandments from the walls of public buildings. Israel, by not bucking the crowd and by becoming like them, was sent into captivity. She had forsaken her Lord and Savior for the pleasures of the world; she sold out. Have you sold out?

Prayer

Heavenly Father, it is so easy to go with the flow. Please give me the strength, Lord, to swim against the crowd and to follow Your desires and commands...

August 18

Seven Days a Week

"Then it shall be, if you by any means forget the Lord your God, and follow other gods, and serve them and worship them, I testify against you this day that you shall surely perish."

—Deuteronomy 8:19

It saddens me to see what America is becoming. Sunday used to be a family day. It was a tradition to get up in the morning, go to church as a family, and eat Sunday dinner together. After eating, the day was spent reading, visiting Grandma and Grandpa, playing games, or napping. But stuff has gotten in the way of that family tradition; we have pretty much forgotten God and given ourselves over to the god of pleasure. Football games, baseball games, going to the lake, shopping, and sleeping in have become more important to us than spending Sunday with the Lord; society is suffering because of this.

If we do not know God by spending time with Him, can we grow as Christians? If we do not spend time with our church family, how can we grow as a family? Forgetting to spend time with our church family is often an indicator of how we spend the rest of the week. Are we serving the god of pleasure more than we are serving our God?

Who are you serving today? Tomorrow? Sunday? Ask God to keep you on track with Him seven days a week.

Prayer

Heavenly Father, I am sorry for the times I have not placed You first in my life. Please keep me from being consumed by the gods of this world…

August 19

Only Today

"Choose for yourselves this day whom you will serve."

—Joshua 24:15

Today, Lord, I am sad. I don't know why, but I choose to worship You in spite of it. Today, I give You all of me. Today, I will seek to touch a life for You. Today, I will reflect on the promises You have given to me in Your Word. Today, I will give thanks for every ache and pain I feel. Today, I will remember Your faithfulness to me. Today, I will remember that this is the day You have made, and I will rejoice and be glad in it (Psalm 118:24). Today, I choose to give You my will so that Your will might be done here on earth (Luke 11:2). Today, I will hide Your Word in my heart so that I might not sin against You (Psalm 119:11). Today, I will give You my all, because I am not guaranteed tomorrow—only today.

Prayer

Lord, today I choose to love You with all my heart. Thank You that no matter what mood I am in when I wake each morning, You ignore my mood and are always there for me…

August 20

God's Choice

O Lord, I know the way of man is not in himself; it is not in man who walks to direct his own steps.

—Jeremiah 10:23

"Lord, why do we worry about things we cannot control?" This question came to my mind one morning as I was reading the Bible during my personal devotions. I thought of my husband, Ken, who had several heart attacks a year ago. I tend to worry about him when I am at work or away from home. God reminded me that I was with Ken when he had most of those heart attacks, and I could not do a thing for him! It was God who spared his life and has given him this past year; it will be God who gives him this next year—or not. It is my job to leave Ken in the Father's hands; it is not my job to fret over him.

God's Word tells us that worrying cannot help us in any way (Luke 12:25). Whatever is worrying you today, place it in God's hands and leave it there.

Prayer

Heavenly Father, thank You for taking all of my worries and giving me freedom to live fully in You…

August 21

A Twenty-Four-Hour God

Pray without ceasing.

—1 Thessalonians 5:17

Talk about a great one-liner! And leave it to God to state it! God tells us in this simple command, you pray without ceasing. When I finally realized what that meant, I was forty years into my Christian walk. One day I noticed that I was sending up short prayers to God all day long during everything I did. I was praying as I did dishes, laundry, and other mundane daily chores; I was praying at work as I answered phones, typed, or folded bulletins. Then it hit me: this is what God wants us to do—be in a continual attitude of prayer, regardless of our posture or location! Wow! After all those years, I had finally gotten it!

Bring God into everything you do, regardless of how small it may seem. Prayer is simply talking with God. If you have not developed praying without ceasing, I encourage you to ask God to help you get there. It changes how you handle life.

Prayer

Father, I am so glad You are a twenty-four-hour God! I do not have to wait for office hours or an open sign on Your door. I can send a prayer to You at any time and know that it is heard...

August 22

Nighttime Refreshers

Be angry, and do not sin. Meditate within your heart on your bed, and be still. Selah.

—Psalm 4:4

I used to feel guilty when I would be in bed at night, praying. I felt like I was being lazy by not being on my knees for that prayer time.

One day as I was reading the psalms, a verse stood out that I had probably read many times before, but it did not catch my attention until that day: "Meditate within your heart upon your bed, and be still."

God knows that lying in bed at night is a good time to let our minds reflect on the day. There are no distractions to keep us from reflecting on all that happened throughout the day—the good and precious things and the not-so-good things that we need to make amends for. As God brings to mind those things that we need to change, we need to listen to Him speak to our hearts. Then, as we continue to be quiet, we can thank Him for all He has done and will do in our lives.

Prayer

Precious Lord, talking with You as I lie on my bed brings true rest to my soul. Thank You, heavenly Father, for my nighttime refreshers...

August 23

Good Choices

"Yet you have not listened to Me," says the Lord, "that you might provoke Me to anger with the works of your hands to your own hurt."

—Jeremiah 25:7

We live in a society that likes to "pass the buck." It is always someone else's fault when something goes wrong. We do not want to accept responsibility for our choices and the repercussions of those choices.

God clearly tells us in the book of Jeremiah that we do things by our own hands that cause God or other people to be angry with us; we do things by our own hands that will even cause us harm. If we choose to use drugs, which destroy the brain, we can't blame our friends for pressuring us—we had a choice. If our friends want to break into a house to get something they are too lazy to work for, we have a choice to join them or turn away from that sin. No one can make us do anything; we always have the choice to say no.

With God's help, we can make the right choices in life. All we have to do is remember to ask for His help. Have you asked for His help lately?

Prayer

Heavenly Father, thank You for being my strength in those times when my flesh wants to be weak. Thank You for helping me make right choices…

August 24

New Every Morning

Through the Lord's mercies we are not consumed, Because His compassions fail not. They are new every morning; Great is Your faithfulness.

—Lamentations 3:22–23

Each of us on the staff of my church takes a turn doing devotions for a week. One morning, as I was searching for what God wanted me to share, I found this question by George MacDonald in *Streams in the Desert*: "Have you ever risen early, climbed a hill, and watched God make a morning?"[17] What a beautiful picture: God making a morning! I pictured the sky as God's canvas—pictured Him lovingly brushing the pale hues of pink and blue or the bright oranges of dawn across the horizon.

I reflected on these verses in Lamentations. God's mercies are given to us each day, as fresh, new, and exciting as the morning He makes. Each day we receive new strength, forgiveness, and grace. Each day is a new start and a chance to allow God to work in and through us. Each day gives us a chance to forget what is behind and become new in Christ—to become as beautiful in our character as the morning God makes.

Ask God to help you bask in the beauty of each new day. Thank Him for His faithfulness and for His mercies, which are new every morning.

Prayer

Merciful Father, may I never take for granted the beauty of each new day. Whether it rains or the sun shines, each day is a gift from You…

August 25

A God of Action

Will a man make gods for himself, Which are not gods?

—Jeremiah 16:20

Love of money; love of possessions; love of clothing; love of food; love of gambling; love of sports; love of relationships—all can become gods. When we put anything or anyone before God, that thing becomes our god. We let it dictate and control us. Our lives literally revolve around those things we worship. They even get in the way of worship on Sunday. It is more important for some of us to go to a football game than to spend time in the house of the Lord, corporately worshipping with other believers.

All of these other gods can do nothing for us. They cannot hear us crying in the night; they cannot heal our broken hearts; they did not fashion us or know us before we were born (Psalm 139). Why, then, do we put them above God?

Search your heart today; what god is your true God?

Prayer

I love You, Abba Father. You were with me before I was born, and You will be with me when I die. Thank You for being a God of action...

August 26

Stubborn Children

"But this is what I commanded them, saying, 'Obey My voice, and I will be your God, and you shall be My people. And walk in all the ways that I have commanded you, that it may be well with you.'"

—Jeremiah 7:23

One day I was babysitting two of my young granddaughters. Darian, who was six years old at the time, was sliding down the stairs on her stomach. I asked her to stop before she got a rug burn. Long story short, she got the rug burn. As she was crying and complaining, "It hurts real bad," I explained that I wasn't trying to spoil her fun or be mean when I asked her to stop; I just did not want her to get hurt.

Our heavenly Father wants to do that for us. He gives us rules and guidelines to follow because He loves us and doesn't want us to get hurt. But sometimes, just like the stubborn Israelites and my stubborn granddaughter, we do not listen to the warnings and we go our own ways—and end up getting hurt.

Is there something God is asking you to avoid because it will harm you? Before you get hurt, ask God to give you the strength to obey, so "that it may be well with you."

Prayer

Abba Father, thank You for loving me enough to give me guidelines for my life. I want to be an obedient child, because I love You. Help me to obey when You gently speak to my heart…

_____

_____

_____

_____

_____

_____

August 27

Every Season of Life

"Please inquire of the Lord for us, for Nebuchadnezzar king of Babylon makes war against us. Perhaps the Lord will deal with us according to all His wonderful works, that the king may go away from us."

—Jeremiah 21:2

How like the nation of Israel we believers can sometimes be! When all is going well, we live our lives to please ourselves. We begin to neglect our quiet time with the Lord, miss a church service or two, put off the Bible study we know we should be doing, and God begins to slip into the background of our lives. Then disaster strikes. It may not be the king of Babylon attacking us, but it is something we feel is too big to fight alone. All of a sudden, we are asking God to save us and perform miracles as He did in times past.

I don't know about you, but I don't want to be like Israel and have God set me aside for a season because of disobedience or because I have forgotten what He has done for me in the past. I want fellowship with God in every season of my life: when I cry; when I laugh; when I stumble. I want God in my life whether it is a bed of roses or a running sewer!

Prayer

Thank You for Your faithfulness, Lord. When I get discouraged or tempted, please remind me of Your faithfulness to me in the past and that You will be with me in the present and the future...

August 28

Hate the Sin—Not the Sinner

The wicked prowl on every side, When vileness is exalted among the sons of men.

—Psalm 12:8

I recently read this passage from the psalms and immediately a picture came to mind of the Gay Parade held annually in San Francisco. According to God's Word, homosexuals are sinners (Romans 1:21–28). They are sinners who openly flaunt their sin as they parade around in lavish costumes and are exalted on television and in the newspapers. Sitcoms on television portray gays as normal—it's just another lifestyle. Some states are trying to legalize gay marriages, even though it is against federal law. As long as this wickedness is condoned, moral issues will only worsen.

As Christians, we need to hate the sin and love the sinner; we need to ask the Lord what we can do to turn the hearts of these fellow Americans to God—the God who died for all of us while we were still sinners (Romans 5:8).

Prayer

Lord, You called Yourself a friend of sinners because they need You desperately. Help me to see them with Your eyes and to pray for ways to hate the sin without hating the sinner…

August 29

Joy, Praise, and Honor

Then it shall be to Me a name of joy, a praise, and an honor before all nations of the earth, who shall hear all the good that I do to them; they shall fear and tremble for all the goodness and all the prosperity that I provide for it.

—Jeremiah 33:9

I live in Vacaville, California, which is known as the "City of Peace." My home church is New Hope Christian Fellowship, and our banner proclaims "Bringing hope to the valley." My church has been blessed with a pastor, Ben Randall, who does not back down from a challenge.

Our church had not been able to buy, lease, or rent property in order to expand because of zoning laws that affected only churches and not other organizations. In 2003, New Hope began the fight to have those ordinances changed. As a result of that persistence, God has blessed us not only with seeing the ordinances changed but also with the miracle of seven acres of land on which to build a new church—a place of hope for those who are broken and desperate.

As I was reading in Jeremiah of God's promise to restore Jerusalem, I thought of New Hope. I believe God is going to use our church as a place of joy, praise, and honor in the city of Vacaville. I believe He placed us in our wonderful city for "such a time as this" (Esther 4:14).

Prayer

Father, it is a blessing to watch where You are working and to become a part of that work. Thank You for the excitement I wake with each morning, as I see Your plan unfold for my church in a city of peace…

_____

_____

_____

_____

_____

August 30

Breathe in God

Lord, I have loved the habitation of Your house, And the place where Your glory dwells.

—Psalm 26:8

Do you find it a joy to get up on Sunday morning, expecting to go to church to meet God in all of His glory? King David loved to go to the House of the Lord. He wanted to bask in the glory of God—to breathe Him deep into his soul.

There are people throughout the world who do not have the privilege of openly worshipping. They have accepted Christ as their Savior, but due to persecution in their land they must worship in secret. How sad to see God's people in America taking for granted the privilege of openly worshipping. To celebrate this freedom of public worship, my church has an annual "Church in the Park" Sunday.

As you enter your place of worship this week, close your eyes and breathe in God. Let Him fill you with His glory—and tell Him "Thank You."

Prayer

Lord, I want all of You, in all of Your glory. Thank you for breathing life into me as your child…

August 31

Stumbling Blocks

But beware lest somehow this liberty of yours become a stumbling block to those who are weak.

—1 Corinthians 8:9

My husband, Ken, is a Type II diabetic. He needs to test his blood sugar daily. Recently, it went up to an unhealthy level; as a result, he was not feeling well. I immediately made all of the dietary changes to lower his blood sugar and began to pray that God would help him return to a safe level quickly.

As I was praying, God impressed on me that I was a stumbling block to my husband. I could eat certain foods without any problem; that was no reason to risk Ken's health by having him share a dessert or sweet snack with me. As I thought about this, I began to weep and ask God to forgive me; then I went to my husband and asked for his forgiveness.

Ken's blood sugar is down, and so is my weight—by four pounds! I guess I was being a stumbling block to myself, as well! Is there an area in your life that could be causing someone you love to stumble?

Prayer

Thank You, Father, for the times that You have gently reminded me of my shortcomings and for loving me in spite of them. Please help me be aware of those around me and how what I do can affect them…

September

September 1

Perfect Love

There is no fear in love; but perfect love casts out fear, because fear involves torment. But he who fears has not been made perfect in love.

—1 John 4:18

There are many of God's people bound up in fear because of past sins. They cannot function as fully as God wants them to when they are paralyzed by fear. Some sins they may have committed themselves; others may have been done unto them. Either way, they feel shame and responsibility for the sin.

Whether your past harbors child abuse, drug abuse, alcoholism, adultery, abortion, or any other shameful occurrence, God loves you! He loves you with a perfect love, dear child! With that perfect love comes forgiveness, mercy, and grace. And perfect love drives out the fear, the shame, the ugliness, and the paralysis of the hurts in your life. Let the perfect love of God drive away the fear in your life, so that He can use you to do the things for which He created you.

Prayer

If you are bound up in fear by a past sin, replace your name for Jacob in the following verse and claim it for yourself: "Do not fear, O Jacob my servant, for I am with you" (Jeremiah 46:28, NIV)…

September 2

Sweet Words

You have tested my heart; You have visited me in the night; You have tried me and have found nothing; I have purposed that my mouth shall not transgress.

—Psalm 17:3

I am in control of my mouth. I can choose to not speak words that belittle or condemn. God provided me with a mind in order to think before I speak—weigh my words before I let them fall on listening ears. Harsh words may be forgiven, but they often are not forgotten and can leave deep scars.

At a women's retreat this past fall, I was praying with a young lady who had come forward for prayer at the end of the service. She was crying, so I cradled her in my arms as I whispered the words sweet baby. Little did I know the impact those two words would have on her! How many times had she heard words that were cruel, belittling, and destructive? Her story broke my heart. I resolved right then to choose that my mouth will not sin—that my words will encourage, edify, and lift up those around me. Can you make the same resolution today?

Prayer

Father, I want to use my mouth as an instrument of Your peace that allows only sweet notes to come forth. Thank You for the words You gave me to pray over my "sweet baby"…

September 3

Armed with Strength

For by You I can run against a troop, By my God I can leap over a wall.
—Psalm 18:29

Philippians 4:13 is one of those scriptures I think most Christians have memorized: "I can do all things through Christ who strengthens me." As I was reading the psalms this morning, I read Psalm 18:29 and received a wonderful visual of Philippians 4:13. With God's help I can run against a troop and leap over a wall! Since I am not very tall, I would really need a lot of help attempting either task! I closed my eyes and actually pictured myself going into battle: I pictured the invisible army around me; I pictured the victory through God's strength. Then I pictured the insurmountable wall in front of me—the task I couldn't complete on my own. God reached His hand down to me; I grabbed it, and He pulled me up and over the wall. I had done it! There truly is victory in Jesus when we rely on His strength and His alone.

Prayer

Father God, it is truly You who arms me with strength and makes my way perfect (Psalm 18:32). Thank You for loving me enough to give me strength when I am weak…

September 4

Without Shame

Indeed, let no one who waits on You be ashamed.

—Psalm 25:3

"Shame on you!" How many times as a child did you have a finger shaken in your face as those exact words were being spoken? When my mother would catch me saying something naughty, teasing someone, or just being mean to a sibling, that "shame on you" made me feel about two inches tall. But praise God—because of the hope we have in Him, we don't need to feel shame. When we do something outside of God's will or character, He will do whatever it takes to get our attention. He might gently nudge us, or it might require something more drastic, but He never shakes His finger and says "shame on you." Like the prodigal son who was welcomed home with open arms by his father (Luke 15:11–24), God opens His arms widely, forgives us, and welcomes us home. His forgiveness and unconditional love give us the assurance that each day is a new beginning for Him and in Him.

Prayer

Heavenly Father, thank You for loving me unconditionally. You always welcome me home with open arms when I come to You asking for forgiveness. You give me grace to walk in the newness of You each day, without shame…

September 5

Behold the Beauty

One thing I have desired of the Lord, That will I seek: That I may dwell in the house of the Lord All the days of my life, To behold the beauty of the Lord, And to inquire in His temple.

—Psalm 27:4

I am a poet at heart, so I really enjoy reading the psalms. King David loved to be in the house of the Lord and frequently wrote a song or poem about his love of God's dwelling place. Each time he went to the temple, he wanted to behold the beauty of the Lord and seek God's will for his life.

As I read Psalm 27, I wanted to be as passionate about being in God's presence as King David was. I wanted to go to my local "temple" and bask in the beauty of the Lord as I sought His will for my life. I have that opportunity every Sunday, if I will avail myself of it. I can choose to go and just fill a seat, doing my Christian duty, or I can go to church expecting to meet God in a new way and asking Him what He wants to do with my life as a willing vessel in the coming week.

Are you a "pew filler," or do you go to church expecting great things? Ask God to examine and speak to your heart, and then make any changes He asks you to make.

Prayer

Lord, You are the reason I wake each morning with a song in my heart. As I worship You in Your corporate dwelling place each Sunday, remind me that my body is your dwelling place (1 Corinthians 6:19) each day of the week and remind me to take Your beauty with me wherever I go…

September 6

Truth Revealed

And all the people went their way to eat and drink, to send portions and rejoice greatly, because they understood the words that were declared to them.

—Nehemiah 8:12

When the meaning of God's Word is revealed to you personally, it is so exciting! You may have read a verse several times before, and then one day God opens your eyes and shows you an application relevant to a situation you are going through.

With understanding comes the ability to make the necessary changes in our lives. God loves to reveal Himself to us; He can only do so when we are in the Word daily. The more we read the Bible and pray for understanding, the clearer we hear God's voice as He reveals truth.

Take time right now to thank the Lord for the understanding He has already given you; then wait with excitement for the new truths He will reveal as you seek more of Him.

Prayer

Precious Lord, You are the joy of my life. Thank You for the understanding You give to me so that I can live a life pleasing to You. You truly are my reason for living…

September 7

God Always Provides

I have been young, and now am old; Yet I have not seen the righteous forsaken, Nor his descendants begging bread.

—Psalm 37:25

My mother was a stay-at-home mom until all nine of her children were in school. Raising nine children on one income must have been very hard on my parents. Yet none of us ever did without anything that was necessary. There was always plenty of good food, because Dad had a garden, raised chickens, geese, rabbits, and pigs, and was a hunter. Mom taught us how to can or freeze things to get us through the winter. When times were tight and it didn't seem as if there would be enough money for a pair of shoes or a new coat, God always provided.

Not only did we not do without the things we needed, but we also had our mother at home with us. I remember her reading the Bible and praying with us before school each morning. Because of parents who raised us in righteousness, we never went without our daily bread—in more ways than one.

Prayer

Father, I thank You for the gift of my godly parents. Because of them, I know Your love and provision. I truly have been young and now I am old; You have never failed to provide for my needs and have given me many of my wants, as well…

September 8

Healed by Touch

Now when the woman saw that she was not hidden, she came trembling; and falling down before Him, she declared to Him in the presence of all the people the reason she had touched Him and how she was healed immediately.

—Luke 8:47

Marilyn Hontz made a powerful statement in her book *Listening for God*: "But when you do touch Jesus through prayer, his power goes out to you."[18] She explained that just as the woman who had bled for twelve years was healed simply by touching the hem of Jesus' garment, so too can we receive the power of Jesus as we touch Him through prayer in faith, believing. Marilyn wanted to "just get close to you [Jesus] so I can touch you."[19] Her heart's desire was to be so intimate with Jesus that she could touch Him through prayer anytime she needed healing or His power to flow through her.

I want that intimate relationship—don't you? As we daily read the Word and commune with Jesus through prayer, intimacy grows; as we touch His garment, we are healed—emotionally, mentally, physically and spiritually.

Prayer

Thank You, Lord, for the intimate moments I have with You. When I reach out and touch You, healing comes to my heart, my body, and my soul…

September 9

Slippery When Wet

But as for me, my feet had almost stumbled; My steps had nearly slipped.
—Psalm 73:2

Can you remember a time when you were walking on a wet or snowy sidewalk and you slipped and almost fell? You know the feeling: Your heart pounds wildly in your chest as you think of what could have happened to you if you had fallen.

I remember walking with a friend some years ago when I actually did slip and fall on a wet sidewalk. Fortunately, I did not severely damage the knee I fell on. But I do know that from that day forward, I was very careful to go around that wet spot on the sidewalk. To this day, when I go by that spot I remember my fall.

God would like us to learn just as quickly in the spiritual realm as I did in the physical realm. He wants us to identify the areas in our lives that could cause us to slip and then ask Him to help us avoid them. Is there a wet spot in your life?

Prayer

Lord, thank You for the times You kept my feet from slipping; more importantly, thank You for the times I did fall and You gently picked me up, forgave me, and cradled me in Your arms…

_____
_____
_____
_____
_____
_____

September 10

Inward Assurance

Then he said to them, "Go your way, eat the fat, drink the sweet, and send portions to those for whom nothing is prepared; for this day is holy to our Lord. Do not sorrow, for the joy of the Lord is your strength."

—Nehemiah 8:10

How does one explain to an unbeliever the peace and joy that can be in a person's life even when "all hell breaks loose"? I think Joyce Meyer says it best in her book *Knowing God Intimately*: "But happiness is based on what is happening at the moment, while joy is based on an internal assurance independent of outward circumstances."[20]

As believers, we have the assurance that God will never leave us or forsake us (Hebrews 13:5). He will be with us in the storm, as He was with Noah (Genesis 7). He will be with us in the fire as He was with Shadrach, Meshach and Abed-Nego (Daniel 3). He will even go into the lions' den with us (Daniel 6).

We may never go through a flood or be thrown into a furnace or lions' den, but we will go through trying circumstances. We can have the assurance of peace on the inside, even when everything is falling apart on the outside.

Prayer

Heavenly Father, thank You for the promise that I will never have to be alone when the darkness surrounds me. I can rest in Your strength; when weeping comes at night, I know I can have joy in the morning because You are with me (Psalm 30:5)…

September 11

While It Is Today

For He says: "In an acceptable time I have heard you, And in the day of salvation I have helped you." Behold, now is the accepted time; behold, now is the day of salvation.

—2 Corinthians 6:2

September 11, 2001. I will never forget where I was on that fateful day that changed America forever. It was 6:00 a.m., and I had turned on the television to watch the news before going to work. The TV screen showed that a plane had crashed into one of the Twin Towers in New York City. As I watched, a second plane was deliberately flown into the second tower! I sat, mesmerized, watching helplessly. The announcement soon came that the Pentagon had also been attacked; by now we knew that this was a planned attack on our country by someone who was using our own planes and citizens as weapons. A fourth plane had been diverted from its target (believed to be the White House) by brave passengers and crashed in rural Pennsylvania.

I could hardly believe my eyes when the two towers began to crumble. As I fell to my knees on my living room floor, I sobbed, "All those people, all those people!" How many were believers? How many went home to be with the Lord?

We are not guaranteed a tomorrow; therefore, today is the day of salvation. We must share God's message while it is still today.

Prayer

Precious Father, please remind me daily that today may be the last day I have to share the gospel. Do not let me be timid in sharing Your message of salvation to a lost and dying world...

_____

_____

_____

_____

_____

September 12

Why Me?

Blessed is the man You choose, And cause to approach You, That he may dwell in Your courts. We shall be satisfied with the goodness of Your house, Of Your holy temple.

—Psalm 65:4

What a privilege to be chosen by God! His Word says it is He who chooses us and gives us the desire to "Enter into His gates with thanksgiving, And into His courts with praise" (Psalm 100:4). I know there have been times when I didn't want to go to church, but I went anyway. Those were also the times when God would bless me in a powerful way. I believe that is His way of rewarding my obedience!

Sometimes the fact that He chose me overwhelms my heart and I weep. Why did He choose me—a plain, ordinary woman? I am reminded in His Word that He chose me because He loves me with an everlasting love (Jeremiah 31:3). That is one of the reasons I go to church on Sunday—to be reminded of all the reasons God loves me.

Prayer

Precious Lord, I want to be full of Your goodness. Please fill me with Your love and grace. Let each day be a new gift from You and a reminder of why You chose me to be Your child…

September 13

Achy Bones

There is no soundness in my flesh Because of Your anger, Nor any health in my bones Because of my sin.

—Psalm 38:3

In Psalm 38, King David was asking the Lord to not rebuke him in anger for his sins. David was basically feeling God's discipline in a physical way—he ached to the very core of his bones.

As I was reading the end of Psalm 38:3, I saw an application for this verse that I had not seen before. A friend of mine had recently told me that when she ate too many sweets, the bones in her body actually ached. As a result of her sin of consuming too much of a good thing, her bones paid the price.

When we make choices in any area of our life that result in sin (overindulgences are sin), we grieve our heavenly Father; we also have to pay the price for that sin. By simply changing our physical or spiritual diets, we could eliminate many diseases of the body and soul. Are your bones aching from sin in your life?

Prayer

I am so guilty of overindulging, Lord! Please forgive me of my sin and help me to make better choices that affect my body and my mind…

September 14

The Empty Hole

They will throw their silver into the streets, And their gold will be like refuse; Their silver and their gold will not be able to deliver them In the day of the wrath of the Lord; They will not satisfy their souls, Nor fill their stomachs, Because it became their stumbling block of iniquity.

—Ezekiel 7:19

I once heard it said that in each of us there is a God-sized hole that only He can fill. God created us for fellowship with Him, and there is absolutely no other thing on earth that can fill that hole. We try to fill it with the things money can buy: new cars, designer clothes, and large bank accounts—you name it. Joyce Meyer, in her book *Knowing God Intimately*, put it this way: "If God created us to need Him, and if we try to live as if we don't, how can we ever be filled?"[21]

We can never be satisfied with the things of the world that often become stumbling blocks. Ask God to completely saturate your soul so that your hunger is satisfied and that empty place in your heart is filled.

Prayer

Oh, how I must grieve You, Lord, when I forget You are the only thing that can quench my thirst or fill my soul. I ask right now for You to completely fill me so that I overflow onto others…

September 15

Stomachaches

And He gave them their request, But sent leanness into their soul.

—Psalm 106:15

I am a junk food junkie; I especially like cookies and peanut M and M's. One day at work this past Christmas I really overdosed on sugar. I had been abstaining from sweets so that I could kick the sugar habit. Then along came Christmas with all of the homemade goodies people brought into the office; out the door went my resolution to not eat sugar. As a result, I became sick to my stomach.

This incident reminded me of how God sometimes allows us to have something we whine for even though He knows it is not good for us. It may be a new car that straps our budget, a relationship that is outside of God's will, or a treat that harms our health. He gives us our desire, but we have to pay the price.

My one-day binge reminded me to thank God for sometimes saying no when I whine about something I want. In His wisdom He knows what my stomach can handle.

Prayer

Abba Father, thank You for the times Your answer has been no to a request I have made. You are my daddy who watches out for me because You love me…

September 16

Not Ready

"I still have many things to say to you, but you cannot bear them now."

—John 16:12

Spiritual growth is like physical growth: we all grow and learn at different speeds. As a baby I walked at nine months. My sister Kathy walked at twelve months.

I had been a born-again believer for forty-two years before I experienced the joy of living fully in the Spirit. Why did it take this length of time before I experienced complete joy in Him when others receive it almost immediately? I was not ready for it any sooner. There were things God needed to teach me—things I had to experience before He could fill me completely with His Spirit. Now that I have experienced that total joy, I never want to be without it. Even when my day is going wrong, I handle it in a different way. I am so thankful He has filled my life, and I can truly say that the joy of the Lord is my strength.

Prayer

My joy is complete because You have filled my life, Father. Please help me to continue to grow in You so that You can reveal new things to me each day…

September 17

Out of the Heart

Keep your heart with all diligence, For out of it spring the issues of life.
—Proverbs 4:23

I remember as a young wife and mother how I used to watch soap operas on television. My husband would laugh and say if he didn't watch the show for three months he could pick the story up again without missing a beat because they were so predictable. This made me angry. But when I realized how my life was being affected by these shows, I had to stop watching them.

My life was going down the drain because I was filling my mind and heart with garbage. "Our destiny, or the outcome of our life, actually comes from our thoughts," wrote Joyce Meyer in *Knowing God Intimately*.[22] I needed to start filling my life with good things to read, watch, and think about. As I began to do that and returned to the things of God, my life began to reflect those changes.

Prayer

Precious Lord, thank You for the purity in my life that comes from keeping the ordinances in Your Word. Help me to spiritually evaluate the things I allow into my life because they affect who I become…

September 18

Blessings of Kindness

We have thought, O God, on Your lovingkindness, In the midst of Your temple.

—Psalm 48:9

There are times during church services when my throat swells with so much emotion while singing worship songs that I have to stop singing. I am overwhelmed by the thought that God loves me and showers me daily with His goodness. There is something about worship that unleashes an outpouring of the Holy Spirit within me that makes me want to shout out the goodness of the Lord.

I am so thankful that God showers me with His blessings, not only on Sunday but on every day of the week. What blessings are you thankful for? Whisper thanks to God for them as you enter your place of worship this week.

Prayer

My life has been showered with blessings from You, heavenly Father. From You come all the good things of life…

September 19

Under His Wings

He shall cover you with His feathers, And under His wings you shall take refuge; His truth shall be your shield and buckler.

—Psalm 91:4

One morning, after reading Psalm 91 during staff devotions, Eric Houser (the youth pastor of my church) shared with the rest of us an interesting fact he learned while hiking on Mount St. Helens in Washington. A plaque located on the side of the trail informed hikers that while cleaning up after the May 1980 eruption of Mount St. Helens, crews found a dead bird with its wings spread wide. As they lifted the bird, her chicks came out from beneath her wings, completely unscathed. She willingly gave up her life to save her babies.

What a precious visual for us as believers! Pastor Eric compared it to how Jesus willingly gave His life for us so that under the shelter of His wings we can experience salvation. We are not only saved from an eternity in hell but protected during the storms of life when circumstances erupt around us. As we choose to remain under Jesus' protection, no matter what may come our way, we are safe because He is with us.

Are you under the shelter of His wings or have you chosen to face the storm alone?

Prayer

I am so thankful, Lord, for the times Your sheltering wings have kept me safe from harm. Thank You for the gift of Your sacrifice so that through Your death I can experience eternal life…

___

___

___

___

___

September 20

Turn Messes into Ministries

And we know that all things work together for good to those who love God, to those who are the called according to His purpose.

—Romans 8:28

There are things that happen in our lives that do not seem fair. We may even ask God, "Why did you let this happen to me?" We live in a fallen world, and we undergo certain things because we live in a fallen world. But as Christians, God can help us overcome bad things and use our experiences for good, helping others who may have been hurt in the same way. In her book *Knowing God Intimately*, Joyce Meyer writes, "If you ask Him to do so, He will take your mess and turn it into your ministry."[23] People who were once in pain start the most effective ministries because they can comfort others as God comforted them (2 Corinthians 1:4). They know firsthand everything involved in the healing process.

If you are in pain because of something that has happened to you, seek help from those who once walked in your shoes. They know how you feel.

Prayer

Precious Father, thank You for the hurts You have healed in my life. I know You want me to walk alongside others and help lift them up as You have lifted me up. Give me an opportunity to help someone who is hurting…

September 21

God's Unfailing Love

Show Your marvelous lovingkindness by Your right hand, O You who save those who trust in You From those who rise up against them.

—Psalm 17:7

Have you ever heard the expression "Feet, don't fail me now"? Well, I remember a time in my childhood when I really didn't want my feet to fail!

I grew up in the country, and when the weather was nice, several of us would ride our bicycles approximately seven miles to school. There was one farmhouse we had to pass where two German shepherds would chase us. As we approached the house, we would pedal as fast as we could to gain enough speed to outrun the dogs. One morning as we reached the house, it wasn't my feet that failed me—it was my bicycle chain that broke! I felt my heart beating wildly in my chest as I saw those dogs getting closer and closer! Just as I was sure that I would be dog food that day, the owner whistled and the dogs gave up the chase.

Psalm 17:7 reminds us of God's marvelous love for us. When our feet want to quit or our equipment breaks down, God is always there for us. Whether the problem is as small as a broken bicycle chain or as big as the loss of a job, when our hearts begin to pound and the enemy gets closer, God whistles, the enemy flees, and we are reminded that God is in control.

Prayer

Lord, there are many times I have been chased by the enemy and have forgotten that You were right there with me. Thank You for showing me unfailing love every day of my life. Please remind me to ask for Your protection daily…

_____

_____

_____

_____

_____

September 22

Set Up to Upset

Be sober, be vigilant; because your adversary the devil walks about like a roaring lion, seeking whom he may devour.

—1 Peter 5:8

All of us who work outside of the home have something at our place of employment that can set us off, even when life is going great. Mine is the copy machine in the church office where I work.

One of my responsibilities each week is to type and copy the Sunday bulletin. Yesterday, as I was running the copies, the copy machine quit in the middle of the job. This would have been okay if we hadn't been having so many problems already and were on our third copier in three years. The day was already hectic, and I wanted to scream! But I remembered something I had read recently in *Knowing God Intimately*: "If God's glory is shining through your life, Satan will set you up to upset you every chance he gets!"[24] I decided right then that Satan was not going to win this round! At that very moment, my coworker Patty Potts came to my rescue and offered to help me print the bulletins the old fashioned way—on our printers, one side at a time. The job was completed before I left, the copier got fixed sooner than expected, and Satan took a back seat that day.

Prayer

Heavenly Father, thank You for reminding me that I am in control of how I react to the situations in my life. I can give in to my natural human reactions and let Satan gloat, or I can ask You to calm my spirit and watch Satan flee…

September 23

Follow Through

Pay what you have vowed—better not to vow than to vow and not pay.

—Ecclesiastes 5:4–5

My desk at work is right in the flow of traffic, so I am able to speak with many people during the course of a day. This morning a gentleman stopped by my desk to give me some papers for one of the pastors; we began to chat about praying for people. He said that he is learning to stop and pray immediately when someone asks for prayer, because he does not want to forget to do it when he tells someone he will pray for them.

I was reminded of God's Word in Ecclesiastes where we are told it is better to not promise to do something than to promise to do it and not follow through. God also tells us to let our yes be yes and our no be no (Matthew 5:37).

I don't know about you, but I needed right then to ask God to forgive me for those times when I failed to do things I had promised to do. If you need a little forgiveness, take a moment right now and go to God.

Prayer

Lord, I know how much it means to me to know I can count on someone. Please help me not to forget to follow through when I tell someone I will do something for them…

September 24

Seasonal Fruit

He shall be like a tree Planted by the rivers of water, That brings forth its fruit in its season, Whose leaf also shall not wither; And whatever he does shall prosper.

—Psalm 1:3

There are many times in ministry when it feels as if we are not seeing any fruit from our endeavors. During those times, it is easy to become discouraged if we do not remember there are seasons for fruit bearing.

When we go grocery shopping and are unable to find some fruits on the shelves because they are out of season, do we get discouraged and say we are never going to buy that fruit again? No, we simply wait until the months come around when the fruit is once again available. We should have the same attitude when fruit from our ministries is "out of season." God wants us to continue to water, fertilize, pull weeds, prune, and tend the soil, growing deep roots, until it is time for the fruit to be produced once again. There is always a season to bear fruit in God's kingdom, so never give up, dear friend.

Prayer

There are so many discouraging times in life, Lord. Please help me to never give up when I don't see fruit. Let me tend my gardens and wait patiently for the harvest to ripen…

September 25

High Standards

Lord, who may abide in Your tabernacle? Who may dwell in Your holy hill?

—Psalm 15:1

God wants His children to have a standard of living that enables them to enter into the Lord's house blamelessly. We are encouraged to walk in righteousness, to speak truth, to treat others with respect, to not take up a reproach against our friends, to despise those who are evil, to not take a bribe against the innocent or use our money to unfairly take advantage of those in need by charging interest (Psalm 15:1–5). Wow! That is a pretty high standard. But God gives us the ability to live such lives through the blood, forgiveness, and righteousness of His Son, Jesus.

As you enter your place of worship this week, take a moment to thank the Lord for the privilege of being able to dwell in His House. What an awesome gift!

Prayer

I am so blessed to be Your child, Father, and to be able to come to Your house in freedom. Thank You for the forgiveness I find through Your Son. May I always walk in the paths of righteousness for Your name's sake (Psalm 23:3)…

September 26

House Rules

Open my eyes, that I may see Wondrous things from Your law.
—Psalm 119:18

My husband loves to "channel surf." Whenever we watch television together, I have to be prepared to have the channel changed as soon as I get interested in something. But one evening, we were both intrigued by a show called "Super Nanny" and watched the entire show. A qualified nanny goes into a home with unruly children and spends a week trying to help the parents learn to control them. The first thing the nanny does is set up a routine—rules for the home. What an amazing change takes place in the behavior of everyone in the home as these rules are put into practice!

As I was reading Psalm 119:18, I was reminded of how God's law does the same thing for us as Christians. When our eyes are opened to the wonderful things that can take place in our lives as we obey God's law, or standards, we enjoy living by those rules. Our lives become peaceful, our homes become orderly, and we can be the children that our "heavenly nanny" desires us to be.

Prayer

Heavenly Father, thank You for the guidelines You have given me to help me become a child You are proud of. When I live by Your rules, there is truly peace in my home—physically and spiritually…

September 27

A Gentle Whisper

...and after the earthquake a fire; but the Lord was not in the fire; and after the fire a still small voice.

—1 Kings 19:12

It would be much easier to hear God's voice if it were always loud, but it isn't; sometimes we don't even recognize it.

Elijah was hiding in a cave from Jezebel when she was seeking to destroy him for killing all of the prophets of Baal. God told Elijah to leave the cave and go up on the mountain to wait for His direction. A great wind shook the mountains—God was not there; an earthquake caused the ground to tremble—God was not there; a fire burned—God was not there. God finally showed Himself to Elijah in a still small voice—a voice that Elijah recognized because he knew God intimately. God gave Elijah instructions to leave the cave—a place of safety—to continue the work He had called Him to do.

Has God been whispering to you, but you weren't sure it was Him? Or maybe you have not wanted to leave your place of safety, so you discounted that gentle whisper. Plan to spend more time with God—to recognize His voice and feel safe doing His will.

Prayer

Lord, sometimes I expect a loud rumble or roar when You want me to hear You. But many times it is only when I sit quietly before You that I hear Your gentle voice, whispering instruction for my life…

_____
_____
_____
_____
_____
_____
_____

September 28

Beautifully Orchestrated

He will not be afraid of evil tidings; His heart is steadfast, trusting in the Lord.

—Psalm 112:7

Bad news. None of us want to hear it; all of us experience it. How we deal with the bad news depends on how much we trust in God.

One day I received a call from a friend who had just attended the wedding of her grandson, which took place on a Saturday. Arlene could not wait to get home the next day and call her elderly father, who lived in another state, and tell him about the wedding. When Arlene and her husband arrived home that Sunday, on her answering machine was a message that her father had passed away the day of the wedding, but no one could reach the family by phone.

Instead of being resentful that she didn't get the news of her ninety-four-year-old father's death right away, Arlene told me, "God was in control. He allowed the wedding of those kids to not be disturbed by sad news. We are celebrating the good things we remember about Daddy. He lived a good life."

Arlene was not afraid of that sad news, which she knew could have come at any time. Because she trusted in the Lord, she was able to thank God, even in her sadness, because He had beautifully orchestrated everything in the birth of a marriage and the end of a wonderful life.

Prayer

Heavenly Father, thank You for being the Great Conductor of life. You truly orchestrate the events in my life so they play out beautifully. Please help me remember that there is nothing to fear when You are in control…

September 29

Weak Flesh

"Watch and pray, lest you enter into temptation. The spirit indeed is willing, but the flesh is weak."

—Matthew 26:41

How many times have you wanted to do something for the Lord and your flesh got in the way? Fasting is one area where my spirit is willing but my flesh is weak! But God is asking me to go a little further in the discipline of fasting. I have found that when God puts something on your mind repeatedly, He wants your attention in that area.

I have been reading *Celebration of Discipline* by Richard Foster. The discipline of fasting was a normal part of worship in Bible times. Foster says, "More recently a renewed interest in fasting has developed, but we have far to go to recover a biblical balance."[25] God apparently wants me to be more biblically balanced; so, although I have an earthly body that often fails, I have a heavenly agenda and will follow God's call—weak flesh and all!

Prayer

Father, as I fast according to Your calling, keep my mind focused on You. When my body begins to falter, give me Your strength to overcome my weakness…

September 30

Pass It On

Now also when I am old and grayheaded, O God, do not forsake me, Until I declare Your strength to this generation, Your power to everyone who is to come.

—Psalm 71:18

Recently, I was sharing with one of the young women at my church about how blessed I was to see so many of the younger women growing in the Lord and stepping out into ministry. Her comment was that it was only because they had been nurtured, loved, and encouraged by the older women of our church that they were able to step out in obedience.

Although most of us think of Titus 2:4, where we are encouraged as older women to mentor the younger women, a lesser-known Scripture came to my mind. In Psalm 71:18 David asked God to continue being with him when he was old and gray, so that he would be able to pass on to the next generation the knowledge of the power and strength of God. As He did with David, God allows us to experience life in order to pass on lessons we've learned to the younger generation. The longer we live, the more we have to pass on.

Now that I am "older and grayer," I really understand the impact I can have on another person's life and eagerly look forward to mentoring others.

Prayer

Lord, if I do not pass on to others the wisdom You have given to me, it is wasted. Please help me to always be ready and willing to come alongside someone who needs love, encouragement, and guidance…

October

October 1

Heavy with Sorrow

My soul melts from heaviness; Strengthen me according to Your word.

—Psalm 119:28

In October 2000, my twenty-year-old nephew Jeremy was in a near-fatal car accident. He sustained severe head trauma, which caused his brain to swell. Part of the brain had to be removed. My brother Garry and his wife, Debbie, were told there was little, if any, brain activity, and they needed to consider unplugging Jeremy from life support.

Well, my mom is a praying mom and grandma; she went to her knees and claimed God's promise that if she prayed, believing, God would hear her prayers (Matthew 21:22). Mom asked that Garry and Debbie be spared the decision of unplugging their son from life support. She prayed until the sweet scent of flowers filled her bedroom. At the time, there were no flowers in her room; she knew the fragrance was the presence of the Lord, giving her peace and letting her know her prayers had been heard.

The next morning a nurse from the hospital called Garry and Debbie and said that there was brain activity in Jeremy and asked them to come to the hospital immediately. Today, Jeremy is alive, healthy and working. I believe this miracle happened because God heard the prayers of a woman whose soul, although weary with sorrow, was strengthened by the promises in His Word.

Prayer

Precious Lord, thank You for hearing the cries of Your children. Thank You for never leaving or forsaking us, especially when our hearts are heavy with sorrow…

October 2

Expectant Worship

I was glad when they said to me, "Let us go into the house of the Lord."

—Psalm 122:1

According to *The New Strong's Exhaustive Concordance of the Bible* (dictionary of the Hebrew Bible), glad in Hebrew is *sâmach*, which means to "brighten up, cheer up, make merry, or cause to rejoice."[26] Are you brightened, cheered, happy, or merry when you attend your place of worship on Sunday? King David was glad when people even mentioned going into the Lord's house. Maybe it was because he had a close and intimate relationship with the Lord and went to the Temple with expectation.

How is your relationship with God? Do you look forward to spending time with Him in your place of corporate worship? Do you expect to hear from Him? If you cannot say yes, ask God to change you and give you a true desire to spend time with Him in His house. Expect God to meet you there. Prepare ahead by being in the Word and in prayer throughout the week. It won't be long until you find yourself looking forward to spending time in the house of the Lord.

Prayer

I know I am Your temple every day, Lord, but there is something special about being in church on Sunday with other believers. As I hear the words You have given to my pastor each week, fill my heart with joy and gladness…

October 3

Gentle Spankings

Let the righteous strike me; It shall be a kindness. And let him rebuke me; It shall be as excellent oil; Let my head not refuse it.

—Psalm 141:5

None of us like to be rebuked or corrected. When we are, our first tendency is to feel inferior, unworthy, or even lacking in something essential. Sometimes we may even feel we shouldn't be in the position we are in. But God's Word tells us when a righteous man or woman corrects us it is a kindness, and we should accept that correction because it is given in love.

Recently, I was corrected for something that I already knew in my heart had been the wrong decision to make. I began to cry—not because the words were harsh, but because I knew in my spirit that I needed correction. It is my prayer that I will always have people in my life who love me enough to give me a gentle "spank" when it is needed. I also need to be prepared to be the one who gives the "spanking." My goal is to be in the Word so I will have the tools I need when it is my turn to do the disciplining.

Prayer

I thank you, Lord, for loving me enough to discipline me when it is needed. Thank You for those You surround me with who gently rebuke me when it is necessary…

October 4

Wisdom and Understanding

Wisdom is the principal thing; Therefore get wisdom. And in all your getting, get understanding.

—Proverbs 4:7

I have often wondered why the energy of youth is wasted on foolishness. I personally experienced a time of foolishness. I was in my thirties when I allowed myself to be enticed by the pleasures of this world. For seven years I wasted energy on things that will pass away and allowed God to take a back seat. I was not interested in attaining God's wisdom or His understanding. In 1987 the Lord finally "jerked my chain" and drew me back to Himself, and I rededicated my life to Him.

I regret those wasted years when I could have been doing so much for God. But God tells us not to look back with regret. Now I seek His wisdom daily, and I never want to go back to the way I felt when my life was not centered on God. I thank Him for saving me from myself, for never leaving me when I left Him, and for giving me a heart that seeks wisdom, knowledge, and understanding above all else.

Prayer

I do not know what I would do without You in my life, Lord. I want to walk with You every day and every night; I want to know You more and more. Thank You for being in my life...

October 5

The Time Is at Hand

Blessed is he who reads and those who hear the words of this prophecy, and keep those things which are written in it; for the time is near.

—Revelation 1:3

During church staff devotions one morning, we were discussing world events. Nancy Minion, our children's ministry pastor, was telling us about a news story about one of the Latin American countries wanting to bring the United States before a world tribunal. The United States is being accused of "illegal practices" against illegal immigrants. Wow! How can those who are in this country illegally complain about being treated illegally? And what right does the world have to try us for our own laws and regulations? Although this event does not make sense, it does bring the world to a place in history where a one-world government is possible. Nancy stated that she feels we are closer to the end times than we realize.

During my personal devotions the next morning, I opened my Bible to Revelation 1:3, where John tells us "the time is near." It was as if God was affirming that the end is near, and we need to reach as many lost sheep as we can before the Lord's return.

Prayer

Lord, there are many who don't know You. Please give me a boldness to reach the lost while there is still time…

_____
_____
_____
_____
_____
_____

October 6

Poor Choices

The foolishness of a man twists his way, And his heart frets against the Lord.
—Proverbs 19:3

"It's not my fault." Our society reels from the effects of living by this statement. Abuse abounds in many forms because of generations of "It's not my fault." When adulthood is reached, a choice can be made to seek help and rise above the abuse and the harm caused by it, but many are content to continue using excuses that say, "I am like this because of..."

Christians are guilty of doing the same thing. We make choices to marry an unbeliever, make unwise business deals, or purchase large items we cannot afford. Then when life goes sour because of our poor choices, we ask, "Why did God let this happen to me?"

The Bible clearly states that it is our own foolishness that brings about much of the calamity in our lives. Do not rant and rave at God for your poor choices. Accept responsibility and seek the forgiveness He freely offers; allow God to guide you to the path of healing and restoration.

Prayer

Father, I have made some poor choices in the past. Please help me accept the forgiveness You offer. Guide me on the path of righteousness, so that I will make decisions that glorify You...

October 7

Boast in God

The king spoke, saying, "Is not this great Babylon, that I have built for a royal dwelling by my mighty power and for the honor of my majesty?"

—Daniel 4:30

It is easy to remember God when we are struggling in the midst of our trials, tribulations and poverty—we have no one else to turn to. In His loving kindness, our heavenly Father helps us put the pieces of our lives back together. Things get better; life is good. And once again, we forget God and trust in ourselves. The boasting begins as we look at what "we did."

King Nebuchadnezzar could only boast for a short time before God put him in his place (Daniel 4:33). We can only boast in ourselves for a short time before God deals with us. Friend, do not wait to be driven into the wilderness, like King Nebuchadnezzar, before you return to the Lord. Recognize and acknowledge that all you have and all you are come from God; give Him the thanks, the glory, and the honor that are due Him.

Prayer

Precious Lord, everything I have that is good comes from You. Thank You for the gifts You have bestowed upon me and for helping me to become the best person I can be through You...

October 8

Faithful Friend

A talebearer reveals secrets, But he who is of a faithful spirit conceals a matter.
—Proverbs 11:13

My husband, Ken, says that there are three forms of quick communication: telegraph, telephone, and "tell a woman." I get offended when I hear him say those words. One day I asked myself why I felt offended. The answer? Truth hurts.

Sometime in our lives we will talk about someone in a way that is considered gossip. Gossip is telling an untruth about someone or saying something that is hurtful about him or her. It is saying something about a person that you are not willing to say face to face. It is betraying a confidence. God wants all of our talk to be edifying and to build up.

I cannot honestly say that I have always done that with my words. I have had to ask God to forgive me for the times I was a "quick form of communication" and to help me be a faithful friend. How do you stand?

Prayer

Lord, I do not want to be an instrument of sorrow because I have hurt someone with my careless words. As I speak with others, please help me guard my tongue. Let no words come forth that are not from You…

October 9

Seated on the Throne

As the deer pants for the water brooks, So pants my soul for You, O God. My soul thirsts for God, for the living God. When shall I come and appear before God?

—Psalm 42:1–2

It happened October 9, 1999, at a campground called Wolf Mountain. I was attending my church's annual women's retreat and was having my free time. I took my Bible and writing materials and sat down on an old wooden merry-go-round near the edge of a small brook. As I was thinking about the events of the morning, a young deer silently approached the water and began to drink. I thought of Psalm 42 and how my desire was to drink from God and quench my spiritual thirst the way this deer refreshed itself at the water's edge.

As I glanced around my surroundings, I saw it: a throne carved into an old tree stump. I had almost missed it hiding in the trees. I pictured Jesus sitting on that throne. A lump formed in my throat as I knelt before Him and quenched my thirst.

Prayer

Lord, I love You! Thank You for being my King, seated on the throne. Thank You for the glory I see in Your creation…

October 10

My God and Me

Let my prayer be set before You as incense, The lifting up of my hands as the evening sacrifice.

—Psalm 141:2

I grew up in a conservative Wesleyan Church in New Jersey. There were very strict rules about dress, jewelry, makeup, movies, dancing, and even ways to worship.

I did not experience the freedom of lifting my hands in worship until I began going to the church I now attend. At first it was uncomfortable for me to see all those hands lifted during worship. But as I studied the Word for myself, I began to understand how God viewed the lifting of hands. He sees it as an "evening sacrifice." I am sending up sweet incense to the Lord when I send up my prayers; with hands lifted high, I sacrifice my will to my Father.

I now have a new freedom when I enter into worship. I can lift my hands and not worry about who is sitting next to me or what they think. In a room full of people, I can close my eyes and enter into a deeper time of worship—just my God and me.

Prayer

Thank You, Abba Father, for the freedom I find in Your Word. As I study Your precepts and learn more about Your ways, it is easier to please You when I enter into a time of worship…

October 11

Timely and Wise

He who answers a matter before he hears it, It is folly and shame to him.

—Proverbs 18:13

What are the qualifications for being a good listener? I'm sure you can think of many, just as I can. The Bible gives us one qualification that is as clear as can be: do not answer a matter until you hear it completely, because you could end up looking foolish. Simply put, do not go ahead of the conversation in your mind, formulating your answer before hearing the entire matter. To answer too quickly can result in giving wrong or untimely advice. God says in Proverbs 18:13 that answering before a matter is completely explained can lead to our shame; we could end up with egg on our faces.

Jesus was slow to speak and weighed His words carefully. As His followers, we should do the same. In your desire to help a friend in need, do not be too quick to solve the problem. Take a moment to ask God to help you give an answer that is timely, wise, and from the Lord.

Prayer

Lord, I have had times when I answered too quickly when a friend came to me for advice. Thank You for taking control of the conversation and turning what could have been a disaster into a mistake that I was forgiven for making…

October 12

The Rottenness of Envy

A sound heart is life to the body, But envy is rottenness to the bones.

—Proverbs 14:30

Someone you know has just accomplished a task that you have been dreaming of doing for years. Instead of being glad for that person, envy and jealousy form a knot in your stomach and you want to scream, "It should have been me!" Immediately you are ashamed of yourself and your reaction; you hug that person and congratulate them. But as the day continues, the ugly feeling hangs on; it does feel like rottenness in your bones. What do you do? You ask God to forgive you for those feelings of envy. You ask God to remove the churning in your stomach and help you to accomplish your own dream. You voluntarily lay down the envy and pick up the peace that God desires for you to have as one of His children. Clothed in that peace, you continue the work God has called you to do, and someday there will be words of congratulations expressed to you for a job well done.

Prayer

Heavenly Father, I do not like the ugly feeling envy produces in me. Whenever it tries to rear its ugly head, please crush the envy beneath Your feet. I want a heart that is flooded with Your peace…

October 13

Childlike Faith

"Assuredly, I say to you, whoever does not receive the kingdom of God as a little child will by no means enter it."

—Luke 18:17

Several years ago, I went to church with a friend whose husband was in the Air Force. They were living in a rented house in town because there was nothing available in base housing. Money was tight, their savings were dwindling, and a house on base seemed very unlikely in the near future.

One night during evening prayers, their four-year-old son thanked Jesus for the house he was going to give them. This prayer continued every night for two weeks: "Thank you, Jesus, for the house you are going to give us on base." When the phone rang at the end of that two weeks and Phyllis was told a house was available for them on base and would be ready in two weeks, she began to cry. She remembered her son's prayer and told me, "He had more faith than I did."

God wants all of His children to come to Him with the same faith as that little boy. In the words of Matthew 18:4, "Therefore whoever humbles himself as this little child is the greatest in the kingdom of heaven."

Prayer

Oh, to have the faith of a child! Father, remind me of this story when I am tempted to give up or see things as impossible. Restore a childlike innocence in me so that I can come to You with a childlike faith…

October 14

Just Enough

Remove falsehood and lies far from me; Give me neither poverty nor riches—Feed me with the food allotted to me; Lest I be full and deny You, And say, "Who is the Lord?" Or lest I be poor and steal, And profane the name of my God.

—Proverbs 30:8–9

Have you ever wondered why God doesn't make all believers wealthy? Think of what could be done for the Kingdom of God if we all were as rich as Bill Gates or Oprah Winfrey! God knows that not all believers would be responsible with great wealth; that is why He had the words of Agur penned in the book of Proverbs. Agur prayed that God would not give him too much money, lest he forget God, or too little money, so that he would resort to theft.

Christians of all eras are the same. If some of us get rich, we get too big for our britches; if some of us become poor, we resort to ungodly practices. Each believer needs to examine his or her own heart and ask God to provide only those resources that he or she can handle. God knows and will provide accordingly. As our faith and responsibility grow, so too will our financial resources grow.

Prayer

Lord, You know what I need for my daily bread. Please provide for my needs as You see fit. Give me no more than I can wisely handle…

October 15

Fashionably Dressed

Strength and honor are her clothing; She shall rejoice in time to come.

—Proverbs 31:25

Fashion trends come and go. Women dress according to those trends, so what is considered appropriate clothing changes from year to year. But there are two things a godly woman should always be clothed in, and they never go out of style: strength and honor. God wants women to be strong and to stand firm for the things of God.

We are the gatekeepers of our homes. We are not to be swayed by the things of this world. Everything we do should be honest and above reproach. Our families and friends watch us to see if our daily walk is in line with our godly talk. If we are clothed in strength and honor, we can rejoice in knowing that when Jesus returns He will find us fashionably dressed and definitely in style.

Prayer

Father, thank You for the guidelines You give us to live by in Your Word. I truly want to be a Proverbs 31 woman, clothed in Your strength and honor…

October 16

God Hears Our Cries

Then he said to me, "Do not fear, Daniel, for from the first day that you set your heart to understand, and to humble yourself before your God, your words were heard; and I have come because of your words."

—Daniel 10:12

I was praying during my quiet time one morning, asking God to give me the right words to use as I wrote in my journal. I wanted to hear His voice and know His direction, because many of the notes I jot down are used later to write devotions.

I finished praying and turned in my Bible to Daniel, where I picked up reading from the day before. As I read that God heard Daniel's words and came to him in response to his heart, I laughed quietly; I knew God was telling me that He had heard my prayer and was answering me quickly. The words I penned in my journal that morning were exactly the words that God wanted me to write.

Prayer

Lord, thank You for the times that You answer my prayers quickly through the reading of the Word; those times are so special to me. Please help me to also remember to not get discouraged when Your answers come more slowly, because Your timing is always perfect…

October 17

The Cares of Life

"But take heed to yourselves, lest your hearts be weighed down with carousing, drunkenness, and cares of this life, and that Day come on you unexpectedly."

—Luke 21:34

God does not want us to be burdened with the cares of this life. Worry can so consume our thoughts that we are oblivious to what is going on around us; Satan can sneak in and slow us down in our work for God before we even realize what is happening.

Recently, I allowed the cares of this world to put me in such a place. Because of health concerns, I became ineffective on the job and allowed my frustrations to make me grumpy with my husband, and my quiet time with God was not quality time. My husband made me realize that I was reacting exactly as the enemy wanted me to react.

When I am burdened with worry, I am not working effectively for God. I asked God to forgive me and then spent the day communing with Him; the cares of the world slowly passed away.

Prayer

Precious Lord, I am so thankful that I can bring my worries to You. Please remind me that I do not have to bear my burdens alone…

October 18

Sacrificial Obedience

Then the king said to Araunah, "No, but I will surely buy it from you for a price; nor will I offer burnt offerings unto the Lord my God with that which costs me nothing." So David bought the threshing floor and the oxen for fifty shekels of silver.

—2 Samuel 24:24

"What does sacrificial giving consist of?" That was a question brought up in my home group when we were studying the topic of stewardship. We then read 2 Samuel 24:15–25. King David went to buy a threshing floor from Araunah the Jebusite so that he could build an altar to the Lord. When the threshing floor was offered as a gift, David turned it down; he didn't want to offer burnt offerings to God that didn't cost him something, so he paid for the threshing floor.

One lady in the group then asked, "How could that be a sacrifice, since he was the king and had all the money he wanted?" Someone else answered that the sacrifice was in building the altar himself. David was the king; he could have had any of his servants build the altar. But the Lord told David to build it (2 Samuel 24:18–19). Because of David's sacrifice of obedience, this site later became the place where the temple in Jerusalem was built. One small sacrificial gift of obedience in the form of an altar led to a place of worship that would always be remembered.

Prayer

Lord, sometimes our sacrificial giving can simply be an act of obedience. Please help me to respond quickly and cheerfully when You call me to sacrifice something that will further Your work…

October 19

Guiding Shepherd

For the idols speak delusion; The diviners envision lies, And tell false dreams; They comfort in vain. Therefore the people wend their way like sheep; They are in trouble because there is no shepherd.

—Zechariah 10:2

Everyone needs to have someone to follow, something to believe in, or a cause to champion. The Bible tells us that the idols in our lives—work, wealth, friends, and possessions—speak lies, and our fortune-tellers give interpretations that are false. We wander around aimlessly, searching for someone to help lift the oppression that presses down from all sides when we have no one to give us guidance.

Jesus wants to be our guide—that shepherd in our lives. He desires us to be as sheep, to know His voice and follow it. We do not need to wander aimlessly in this life when we choose Jesus as our Savior. He will guide us and light our path with truth. He will comfort us. He will always be available when we need direction. He will lift the oppression and set us free! Hallelujah, what a Savior!

Prayer

Heavenly Father, thank You for being my Shepherd. I will never need to wander aimlessly when I stay within Your fold…

October 20

Fine China

Behold, I have refined you, but not as silver; I have tested you in the furnace of affliction.

—Isaiah 48:10

For believers, our time on earth is a time for refining and purifying—a time of preparation for service and eternity. The trials, which are allowed into our lives by God, are part of the refining process, which molds us into the vessels Jesus desires us to be. Every time a "fiery furnace" confronts us, we have a choice: We can complain, whine, and grumble about it, or we can ask God to show us what He wants us to learn from the experience.

I once heard that when a good piece of china comes out of the kiln, the potter "pings" it with his finger. If the china "sings," it is ready for cooling and usage. If the china doesn't sing, back into the furnace it goes. The moral of this story is, sing when God takes you out of your affliction! Otherwise, He will put you back into the fire to be further refined.

Thank the Lord for the events of your life that have been part of making you a pure vessel for Jesus.

Prayer

Precious Lord, thank You for making me a vessel of great value. I am no longer a lump of clay but a piece of fine china in Your Kingdom, designed for a special purpose…

October 21

A Prisoner of Hope

Return to the stronghold, You prisoners of hope. Even today I declare That I will restore double to you.

—Zechariah 9:12

I am in this world but not of this world; therefore, I am a prisoner. But, I am a prisoner of hope! I have hope because Jesus is my Savior; I have reason to rejoice, because one day Jesus will return for me and rescue me from my prison. He is preparing a place for me right now in His Father's house (John 14:1–3). When He returns, I will be freed from the trials and tribulations of this world. I will no longer be a prisoner of hope; I will be a free woman in heaven, living in a mansion prepared for me. And since I don't live in a mansion right now, I certainly will be doubly blessed when Jesus comes to take me home!

Prayer

Thank You, Lord, for the hope I have in You. I am waiting for Your return with great excitement and expectation…

October 22

Temporary Treasures

While we do not look at the things which are seen, but at the things which are not seen. For the things which are seen are temporary, but the things which are not seen are eternal.

—2 Corinthians 4:18

My home Bible study group recently completed a five-week series on stewardship. When the word stewardship is mentioned, most of us immediately think in terms of dollars and cents. But total stewardship involves our time, talents, and spiritual gifts as well as our money.

Many of us have no trouble buying a season pass year after year to a baseball, football, or soccer team's games. But if we are asked to commit to a three-year building pledge to build a larger church, we balk. We will spend five or six nights a week driving kids to ball games, scouts, or school functions, but we cannot spend one night a week in Bible study. We spend double the time on things that are temporary. Things that have eternal value seem to be low on our list of priorities. It is time to check our hearts to see if we are devoting more energy to the seen than the unseen.

Prayer

Lord, please forgive me for placing more value on those things that are temporary than on those that are eternal. Please help me to set priorities in my life that have value in Your eyes…

October 23

Fly Away

So I said, "Oh, that I had wings like a dove! I would I fly away and be at rest."

—Psalm 55:6

King David was burdened with the cares of the world as he wrote Psalm 55. He was filled with fear and actually trembled because of the horrors overwhelming him (Psalm 55:6). As David poured his heart out to God, he expressed his desire to have the wings of a dove so he could fly away—leave it all—and finally rest.

Life can be that way for us sometimes. Our marriages are in shambles, our children are making bad choices, the pressures from work begin to crush us, and we feel as if we can't breathe with the weight of it all; escape is the only thought occupying our minds. Where can we go? To whom can we run? Jesus tells us to cast our cares on Him (1 Peter 5:7). In Matthew 11:28 we are told to "Come to Me, all you who labor and are heavy laden, and I will give you rest."

We don't need to fly away for rest; we need to run to Jesus. Run to Him today, dear friend, and He will give you the rest you desperately need.

Prayer

Father, thank You for the loving arms You wrap around me as I rest upon Your shoulder. I don't need to escape my problems by flying away when I can run to You…

_____
_____
_____
_____
_____
_____
_____

October 24

Cracked Pots

And the vessel that he made of clay was marred in the hand of the potter; so he made it again into another vessel, as it seemed good to the potter to make.

—Jeremiah 18:4

As I was speaking to my mother one day, she shared that she was feeling down for no apparent reason. The longer our conversation went on, the more I began to think she was feeling a bit "useless." My mother has always been a hard worker. Now, at age seventy-five, she has had to retire due to health problems. Staying at home without a "purpose" is beginning to take its toll.

I remembered a story I once heard, which I shared with Mom. There was a man who went to draw water from a well each day, using a cracked pot. Although half of the water would leak out on the trip home, the man had no other pot to use. Soon, flowers began to spring up along the path the man traveled. Their beauty was seen and enjoyed by everyone. Without the water that leaked from the pot, those flowers would not have grown.[27]

I told my mother that she was God's cracked pot, and He would continue to use her if she was willing. She could water things along the way and watch them grow, or perhaps God would even shape her into a brand new vessel. Either way, she has a purpose and a reason to rejoice, because He is using her.

Prayer

Precious Father, I am so glad to be a clay pot in Your Kingdom. Please help me to be the best pot I can be—cracks and all…

October 25

Bread of Life

When the day began to wear away, the twelve came and said to Him, "Send the multitude away, that they may go into the surrounding towns and country, and lodge and get provisions; for we are in a deserted place here." But He said to them, "You give them something to eat."

—Luke 9:12–13

When Jesus was preaching to the multitude in Bethsaida and the day "began to wear away," His disciples approached Him about sending the people into neighboring towns to find food and lodging for themselves. It must have surprised them when Jesus said, "You give them something to eat." Where would they get enough food to feed all of the people? Only five loaves of bread and two fish were available. Jesus then broke that bread and those fish, blessed it, and fed the people (with twelve baskets of food left over!).

Jesus, our broken and blessed Bread of Life, still commands His disciples to feed the multitude (John 21:15). We are to share the gospel and give encouragement to all the hungry people who are placed in our life. I encourage you to look for someone who is hungry for the love of Jesus and feed them with food that will satisfy them for eternity—the Bread of Life.

Prayer

Jesus, thank You for the gift of Your sacrifice on the cross so that I will never hunger again. Please help me to watch for those who are starving for You and need the Bread of Life…

_____

_____

_____

_____

_____

_____

_____

October 26

Be My Daddy

A father of the fatherless, a defender of widows, Is God in His holy habitation.
—Psalm 68:5

As I was reading my Bible one morning, God gave me Psalm 68:5 to share with a good friend of mine. Bobbi is a young believer; she is also a young widow. She did not ask to be single and gets angry sometimes when she is feeling lonely or doesn't have anyone to share things with at the end of the day. Furthermore, her father has also passed away, so she doesn't have a dad to give her advice. Basically, she doesn't have a guy in her life when she really needs one.

God wanted me to share with Bobbi that He has a special place for her in His heart. He wants to be her daddy when she feels alone; He wants to be her defender when she needs someone to protect her and stand up for her. He loves her so much that He has surrounded her with women who are grounded in the Word and can share Scriptures to encourage and inspire her.

Are you in need of a daddy or a defender? Jesus is waiting with open arms; you only need to turn to Him and accept His embrace.

Prayer

Abba Father, I am so glad You are my daddy. You will never leave or forsake me. You will be there when I need a shoulder to cry on…

October 27

A Dose of Jesus

Jesus answered and said to them, "Those who are well have no need of a physician, but those who are sick. I have not come to call the righteous, but sinners, to repentance."

—Luke 5:31–32

Christians have a tendency to surround themselves with other Christians. Although we need other believers for encouragement, for accountability, and for helping us grow in the Word, Jesus reminds us in Luke 5 that healthy people have no need of a doctor; it is the sick who are in need of healing.

Sometimes it is necessary for us to get out of our comfort zone—our church—and attend a family dinner, a company event, or a neighborhood BBQ, so that we can be a light shining in the darkness and administer a "dose of Jesus" to those who are sick. As others begin to see what God has done in our lives, they will want a "shot" of the medicine that has brought healing to us, administered by the Great Physician, Jesus.

Prayer

Heavenly Father, thank You for the healing You have given to me. Remind me to be unselfish and share Your medicine with others, so that they can be healed…

October 28

Without Limit

For He whom God has sent speaks the words of God, for God does not give the Spirit by measure.

—John 3:34

Are you aware that there is something you can have without limit or restriction—and it is good for you? Unlike the list of restricted foods we have while on a physical diet, a spiritual diet contains a list with an unlimited ingredient on it: the Holy Spirit.

God tells us in John 3 that He wants us to have as much of the Holy Spirit as we want; He does not measure it out and say "Enough." As we grow in our walk, we can ask the Spirit to increase His activity in our lives. We can ask Him to empower us with gifts that we were once not ready for because of fear or misunderstanding. There are things we can do through the Spirit that will totally amaze us—things we never dreamed we could do! Ask God to pour more of His Spirit into you, so that you can do amazing things for Jesus.

Prayer

Lord, I want as much of You as I can get! Open my heart to be receptive to everything You want to pour into me…

October 29

A Reflection of Jesus

The law of truth was in his mouth, And injustice was not found on his lips. He walked with Me in peace and equity, And turned many away from iniquity.

—Malachi 2:6

Oh, how I want the law of truth to be in my mouth! As with Levi, who is spoken of in Malachi 2, I want people to believe what I say and value the words of encouragement and counsel I give to them. I want to be known as a woman of peace and righteousness. I want others to say I lived what I talked. I want others to come to Jesus because they wanted what I modeled in my daily life. I want others to want my Jesus.

What do you want others to remember about you? Ask God to help you live a life that will be a testimony of His grace and mercy and a memorial to the righteousness attained by living in Jesus.

Prayer

Lord, thank You for providing me with the tools I need to live a righteous life in Christ. Let who I am be a reflection of You…

October 30

Reap Everlasting Life

For he who sows to his flesh will of the flesh reap corruption, but he who sows to the Spirit will of the Spirit reap everlasting life.

—Galatians 6:8

We've all heard these expressions: garbage in—garbage out; you are what you eat; like father, like son. These are all "truths" about situations that we have control over. God's Word tells us that if we cater to the flesh—the things of this world—we will reap corruption. But if we cater to the Spirit, we will reap everlasting life.

Each of us makes the choice of how we live our life. We can watch soap operas and reality TV, or we can read the Bible, encouraging devotionals, or Christian novels. We can continue in a generational sin, or we can seek godly counsel to help us overcome a pattern of abuse or neglect. We can choose to reap good things by sowing good things.

What habits or patterns are you sowing in your life? Ask God to help you make choices that will reap everlasting life.

Prayer

Heavenly Father, I want to live a life that reaps spiritual fruit. I want what I sow to have eternal rewards. Thank You for guiding me with Your truth…

October 31

Become Contagious

"Thus says the Lord of hosts: 'In those days ten men from every language of the nations shall grasp the sleeve of a Jewish man, saying, "Let us go with you, for we have heard that God is with you."'"

—Zechariah 8:23

God wants us to be contagious Christians. He wants us to live our lives in such a way that other people want to grab on to our coattails and follow us because they see the protection and guidance God provides.

In his book *Becoming a Contagious Christian*, Bill Hybels says, "Although our actions have nothing to do with gaining our own salvation, *they might be used by God to save somebody else!*"[28] It is important that each of us live a life that will attract others. When we reflect peace in the midst of a crisis, others are drawn to us. When we do not worry when life throws us an unexpected curve ball, others are drawn to us. When we turn to Jesus with confidence that He hears our prayers, others are drawn to us.

Are others drawn to you? Are you a contagious Christian?

Prayer

Help me, Lord, to attract others to You. When someone grabs on to my skirt, let me lead him or her to You…

November

November 1

Deaf Ears

"Therefore it happened, that just as He proclaimed and they would not hear, so they called out and I would not listen," says Lord of hosts.

—Zechariah 7:13

You can only turn a deaf ear to God for so long; He then turns a deaf ear to your pleas. Zechariah was sent by God to give instruction to the Israelites. But they turned a deaf ear to Him; they stopped their ears, so they could not hear. If they did not know the law, they would not have to act upon it. God became angry at the Israelites and told them that because they had not listened to Zechariah, His messenger, He would not listen to them when they cried out to Him.

The same thing can happen to us today. When God talks to us through His Word or a fellow believer and we ignore the command, we run the risk of God turning a deaf ear to us. Personally, I do not want to run that risk. Hearing God's voice is essential in my life; can you say the same?

Prayer

Thank You, Father, for the instruction You give me for my life. I always want to hear Your voice. Without the plans You have for me, I would have no purpose...

November 2

Victory Is Ours

"They will fight against you, But they shall not prevail against you. For I am with you," says the Lord, "to deliver you."

—Jeremiah 1:19

Election Day, November 2, 2004, was a day of victory for the evangelical people of America. President George W. Bush stood his ground against Senator John Kerry and was re-elected for a second term as president of the United States of America.

I believe this victory was possible only because God's people said the time for us to be heard is now. The change in America has to begin with us. We must humble ourselves and pray and seek God's face (2 Chronicles 7:14).

God heard His people as they prayed for a righteous man to be placed in office. I believe He was saying to us, "The enemy will fight against you but won't win, because I am with you." What an awesome assurance we have in Christ!

The nation of America wants to return to a land of morals and godly principles. Will the leaders of our land hear our voice? I know God has heard, and for a season of time we have been victorious, and a godly man will lead America.

Prayer

You are faithful to hear the prayers of Your people, Lord. Please remind us that change always begins with us. Thank You for the victory we experience in You…

November 3

Good Things

John answered and said, "A man can receive nothing unless it has been given to him from heaven."

—John 3:27

It is easy to pat myself on the back and say, "Look what I did." In reality, I can do nothing apart from God. He is the one who knew me before I was born (Psalm 139) and had a plan for my life from the very beginning (Jeremiah 29:11). God gave me all of the talents and spiritual gifts that I have, so that I could carry out His plan for my life. When I successfully accomplish something and get a compliment about it, it is okay to say "thank you" and feel good about a job done well. However, I must remember to give God the final credit and glory; all good things come from Him.

Thank God today for the good things He has given to you.

Prayer

Heavenly Father, You have given me more than I ever imagined I would have. You have given me vision and purpose for my life and filled my days with peace and contentment. Thank You for the good things I have been blessed with…

November 4

Chopped Down

"Therefore bear fruits worthy of repentance...And even now the ax is laid to the root of the trees. Therefore every tree which does not bear good fruit is cut down and thrown into the fire."

—Matthew 3:8,10

When we receive forgiveness for our sins, changes in our lives should reflect true repentance. Those changes should allow others to see the fruit of the Spirit in us: love, joy, peace, patience, kindness, goodness, faithfulness, gentleness and self-control (Galatians 5:22). If these qualities are not lived out in our born-again lives, one could doubt whether true repentance occurred.

God is watching each person who professes Jesus as Savior. If He does not see the fruit that exhibits true repentance, He can prune us or "chop us down." According to Matthew 3, He can even throw us into the fire!

Can others see the fruit of the Spirit in you, or do you need a little pruning?

Prayer

Father, please forgive me for the times I do not exhibit Your qualities in my life. I want others to know how much I love You by my actions, not just by my words...

November 5

Satan's Deceptions

Then the devil left Him, and behold, angels came and ministered to Him.
—Matthew 4:11

Satan's number one job in this world is to trip you up and render you useless for the Kingdom of God. He does not want you to lead others to Jesus and will do everything he can to deceive you and lure you away from God. However, you are in good company; the Bible tells us that the devil even tempted Jesus (Matthew 4:1–10). But Jesus did not argue with Satan; He used the Word of God as His only weapon, and Satan finally left.

When you and I are faced with the tricks and deceptions of Satan, we need to remember to fight back with the truth found only in God's Word. Satan will try to trip us up by quoting Scripture (Matthew 4:6). Memorizing Scripture puts the Word of God in our minds, where it is readily accessible, so we can fight the attacks from Satan at any time.

I encourage you to memorize verses that are important to you, so that when Satan knocks on your door you will be ready with an answer. Keep throwing God's Word at him, and he will give up and leave.

Prayer

Lord, You are stronger than Satan and have already won the battle for me. Always remind me to use Your Word as a sword to make the devil flee when times of temptation come into my life…

November 6

As Faithful As Job

Though the fig tree may not blossom, Nor fruit be on the vines; Though the labor of the olive may fail, And the fields yield no food; Though the flock may be cut off from the fold, And there be no herd in the stalls—Yet I will rejoice in the Lord, I will joy in the God of my salvation.

—Habakkuk 3:17–18

I would venture to say that most people have heard of Job in the Bible. He lost everything he had—family, flocks, wealth, and health—and still held tight to his faith in God. But how many of us have heard of Habakkuk? He is one of the minor prophets in the Bible, as there are only three chapters in the book of Habakkuk. One thing stood out to me as I read this book: Habakkuk wanted to be as faithful to God as Job was. He didn't care what he lost in life; he was going to rejoice in the Lord because of his salvation.

Are you able to rejoice in the Lord even when life seems to be grinding you into the asphalt? Total joy in spite of your circumstances can happen when your life belongs to God.

Prayer

Father, when I feel as if I have lost everything, remind me that I will always have You. There is nothing in my life as important as Your love for me. Thank You for the joy of my salvation…

November 7

Loaves of Love

"Or what man is there among you who, if his son asks for bread, will give him a stone?"

—Matthew 7:9

My church has a group of women who call themselves SAM: Supporting All Military. In November 2004, this group of ladies got together to gather shoe boxes full of goodies to send to American troops in Iraq for Christmas. There were ninety-seven men and women in the group that they wanted to bless, but only twenty-five boxes were at the church the morning the ladies came to process them.

I am a staff member at my church, and on my break I went into the room where the women were wrapping the boxes for shipping. The women were concerned that we would not have a box for every soldier. I reminded them of the story in Matthew 7. Would a father give his son a stone if he asked for bread? Hadn't the women specifically asked for ninety-seven boxes? And what about the story of the loaves and fishes in Matthew 14? Didn't Jesus supply enough for everyone to be fed? Where was their faith? They had asked God for a specific number, and He would supply that need. They all agreed to believe that God would provide above and beyond what was needed.

Hour by hour more boxes came in, and by late afternoon the tables were full. The women had received well over the number of shoe boxes needed; they had more than enough "loaves" to go around.

Prayer

Thank You, Lord, for providing for me in every area of my life. When I begin to doubt that You will supply my needs, remind me to go to Your Word and stand on Your promises…

November 8

Serve Until...

"But take careful heed to do the commandment and the law which Moses the servant of the Lord commanded you, to love the Lord your God, to walk in all His ways, to keep His commandments, to hold fast to Him, and to serve Him with all your heart and with all your soul."

—Joshua 22:5

Did you know there is no retirement in God's Kingdom? I cannot find anything in the Bible that says you can retire from God's work when you are exhausted or reach a certain age. Joshua 22:5 says to serve the Lord with all our heart and soul—period. You don't serve until you are tired or reach the age of sixty-five. Moses was actually eighty when God called him to serve!

Has God been nudging you into an area of ministry and you feel you are too old? Accept the call and come out of retirement; the rewards will be awesome!

Prayer

Precious Lord, thank You for not placing us on a shelf marked "useless" when we grow older. There will always be something for each of Your children to do until we draw our last breath here on earth…

November 9

No Lazy People

The soul of a lazy man desires, and has nothing; But the soul of the diligent shall be made rich.

—Proverbs 13:4

It seems as though more and more people want maximum wages for minimum effort. But God wants us to work for what we have. That means there are to be no lazy people in God's Kingdom. As we are diligent in what we do each day, we will be satisfied not only with our work but also with the wages that pay for the food we eat, the homes we live in, and the clothes we wear.

In 2 Thessalonians 3:10, God straightforwardly says, "If anyone will not work, neither shall he eat." That is about as black and white as you can get. When you are tempted to let someone else carry your share of the load, remind yourself of what God wants you to do. Put your back to the task, and enjoy the rewards of a job well done.

Prayer

Heavenly Father, please forgive me for the times I have been content to let others do my work. Remind me of the satisfaction that will come from a hard day's work…

November 10

Will Jesus Find Faith?

"I tell you that He will avenge them speedily. Nevertheless, when the Son of Man comes, will He really find faith on the earth?"

—Luke 18:8

Will Jesus find faith in me when He returns to the earth? I asked myself this question as I was reading in Luke this morning. Jesus had just finished telling His disciples the parable of the widow who repeatedly went to a judge, begging him to plead her case. The judge finally gave in "lest by her coming she weary me" (Luke 18:5). This woman was rewarded for her conviction that the judge would listen if she persevered.

Jesus wants each of His children to come to Him with enough faith to believe that He will answer our persistent pleas for justice, provision, protection, and healing. He wants us to have great faith: the faith of the centurion who asked Jesus to speak healing for his servant sick in bed (Matthew 8:5–13); the faith of the woman who touched the hem of His garment, expecting healing (Matthew 9:20–21); the faith of the four men who lowered their sick friend through a roof for Jesus to heal (Mark 2:3–11); the faith of Abraham, Noah, Mary, and David, who all believed God's promises. Will Jesus find such faith in you or me when He returns?

Prayer

Lord, I want to be found faithful when You return to earth. Help me to hold tightly to Your promises and step out in faith when it is required of me…

November 11

With Authority

...for He taught them as one having authority, and not as the scribes.

—Matthew 7:29

Jesus comes into our lives with authority. He is one with the Father (John 10:30). He has been authorized by God to speak truth—to speak promises that will forever change our lives and set us free (John 8:32).

In Matthew 7 we are told that Jesus astonished the people with His method of teaching; it was unlike anything they had ever heard from the scribes. When Jesus spoke to the people during the feast of the tabernacle, they said that never had a man spoken as Jesus had (John 7:46). The people recognized authority when they saw it.

Jesus wants you and me to recognize His authority in our lives. He wants only the best for us. When we live by His truth, that best is accomplished in us through the power of the Holy Spirit and the authority of Jesus.

Prayer

Thank You, heavenly Father, for the precious gift of the One who has authority to make my life all it can be for You. Please pour into me more of Your Spirit as I draw closer to You through Your Word and prayer...

November 12

Ask Jesus

And behold, a leper came and worshiped Him, saying, "Lord, if You are willing, You can make me clean." Then Jesus put out His hand and touched him, saying, "I am willing; be cleansed." Immediately his leprosy was cleansed.

—Matthew 8:2–3

Have there been times in your life when you wanted a healing touch from Jesus and didn't get it? You wanted a touch, but did you ask for it? Sometimes Jesus is only waiting for us to ask Him for healing or cleansing. He is always willing to touch, heal, and forgive but never invades our life as a dictator. It is our choice to go to Him or not.

The leper approached Jesus in the middle of a crowd and asked for cleansing. We often are afraid to ask even in the privacy of our own home. Is there something in your life that needs a healing touch from Jesus right now? Regardless of where you are at this moment, you can ask Him to touch you, and He will. It is your choice.

Prayer

Heavenly Father, You are my reason for living. I need Your touch today. I need Your forgiveness and grace to sustain me. I need Your love, power, and strength to make me all that I can be in You…

November 13

Love the Unlovable

"But I say to you, love your enemies, bless those who curse you, do good to those who hate you, and pray for those who spitefully use you and persecute you."

—Matthew 5:44

I don't know about you, but I have a hard time loving and praying for my enemies. However, God does not give me a choice in this matter. He wants all of His children—that includes you and me—to love our enemies, bless those who curse us (ouch!), and pray for those who use and despise us. In our own flesh we can't do these things. We want to hit back when we are attacked. It is only the power of the Holy Spirit that enables us to love those who hurt us in body or spirit.

It is easy to love the lovable; Jesus wants us to do the difficult and love the unlovable. Our reward comes from doing the difficult. Ask Jesus to give you His heart, to enable you to love the difficult and unlovable people in your life.

Prayer

Lord, when I want to hurt back, help me to remember how You treated those who inflicted pain on You. You asked the Father to forgive them because they didn't know what they were doing (Luke 23:34). Please give me that same love for my enemies…

November 14

A Strengthening Angel

"Father, if it is Your will, take this cup from Me; nevertheless not My will, but Yours, be done." Then an angel appeared to Him from heaven, strengthening Him.

—Luke 22:42–43

Doing God's will and walking in obedience is hard, especially when everything inside you is screaming to take the easy way out. I have a friend who is walking beside her daughter during a difficult time as this is being written. They are choosing the hard way—God's way—in dealing with a sad situation.

My friend's daughter is unmarried and pregnant, and there are complications with the pregnancy. Tests show that if the baby were carried to full term, life expectancy would be only minutes to a year. Doctors have recommended abortion; God has reminded my friend and her daughter that He is the Creator of life.

Is there fear? Yes. But just as God sent a strengthening angel to Jesus in the Garden of Gethsemane, so too will God send a strengthening angel to my friends as they walk in obedience.

Prayer

Precious Lord, thank You for the strength You surround me with when life seems almost unbearable. Your angels have surrounded me many times during times of crises…

November 15

Help My Unbelief

Immediately the father of the child cried out and said with tears, "Lord, I believe; help my unbelief!"

—Mark 9:24

All of us struggle with believing that Jesus can move mountains or raise the dead. We don't want to struggle with unbelief, but we do. God knew we would need help in this area, so He left a story in the ninth book of Mark to encourage us.

There was a man who came to the disciples and asked them to cast a demon out of his son. When they could not, this father approached Jesus and asked Him if He could cast out this "mute spirit." Jesus answered, "If you can believe, all things are possible to him who believes" (Mark 9:23). The Bible tells us the father cried out, "Lord, I believe; help my unbelief!" You see, he desperately wanted to believe Jesus could heal his son, yet there was the human side of him that needed Jesus to fuel his belief and give it power. We can be the same way.

Ask Jesus to help you overcome any unbelief in your life. If you believe—truly believe—anything is possible.

Prayer

Lord, I struggle with my human frailties. Thank You for providing me with the means to overcome my unbelief and for giving me strength when my faith wavers…

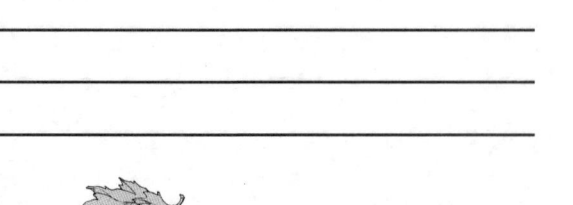

November 16

Are You Ready?

Then He said to them, "Follow Me, and I will make you fishers of men." They immediately left their nets and followed Him.

—Matthew 4:19–20

If Jesus knocked on your door at this exact moment and asked you to immediately drop everything and follow Him, would you do it? I doubt it. Most of us would have a million reasons for not being able to leave right away. But when Peter and Andrew (the first two disciples) were asked to follow Jesus, they dropped everything immediately and followed him. The New International Version Bible says they left at once. They left their jobs, their homes and their families, with no excuses and no looking back.

Jesus wants you and me to love Him so much that when He calls us we will be ready to leave as quickly as those first disciples did. Are you ready for the knock on your door?

Prayer

Heavenly Father, I want to be ready to follow You when You call. Please open my eyes and my heart as I read Your Word for guidance and instruction, preparing myself to be ready at all times…

November 17

Careless Words

"But I say to you that for every idle [careless] word men may speak, they will give account of it in the day of judgment."

—Matthew 12:36

"I hate you!" I remember screaming those exact words at my parents when I was about fourteen years old. Did I really hate my parents? No. Those mean words were spoken carelessly in a moment of anger because I had not been allowed to do something I felt I had to do. By telling me no, my parents were showing me how much they loved me and cared for my well-being; in my selfishness, I hurt them with words I didn't really mean. I can't take back those words, even though I have been forgiven for saying them.

I was reminded in my personal devotions this morning that every careless word I have spoken will have to be answered for. I have been forgiven for saying them, but I will have to give an account for them. Are there careless words you have spoken and need forgiveness for? First, accept the forgiveness; then ask Jesus to help you guard your tongue from speaking careless words.

Prayer

Forgive me, Father, for the words I have spoken that brought pain to others. Please help me to remember to think before I speak, because my words cannot be taken back once they are uttered…

November 18

According to Your Faith

And when He had come into the house, the blind men came to Him. And Jesus said to them, "Do you believe that I am able to do this?" They said to Him, "Yes, Lord." Then He touched their eyes, saying, "According to your faith let it be to you."

—Matthew 9:28–29

How much faith do you have in Jesus? Do you believe He still performs miracles? According to the Bible, the number of miracles we see take place in our lives is in direct proportion to the amount of faith we have in Jesus and His authority to heal and restore.

When everyone around you says, "It can't be done," do you remember that nothing is impossible with God (Genesis 18:13–14)? Or do you think about the time Jesus parted the Red Sea for the Israelites to escape from the Egyptians (Exodus 14:21)? How about remembering the greatest miracle of all, when Jesus rose from the dead in order to make it possible for you and me to receive salvation (Luke 24:1–3)?

If you desperately need a miracle in your life, work on increasing your faith: "According to your faith let it be to you."

Prayer

Lord, thank You for the miracles I have seen take place around me. Thank You for increasing my faith and allowing me to experience more of You in every area of my life…

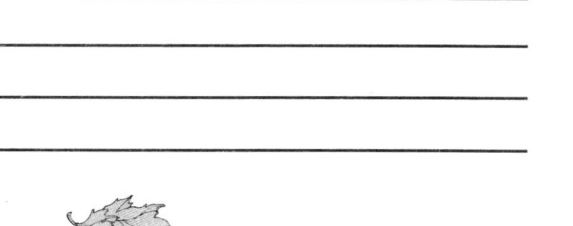

November 19

Stand Still

And Moses said to the people, "Do not be afraid. Stand still, and see the salvation of the Lord, which He will accomplish for you today. For the Egyptians whom you see today, you shall see again no more forever."

—Exodus 14:13

Standing firm or still in times of indecision is difficult for many of us. We want to either lower our heads and charge like a bull right into the middle of a situation or run away from it like a cowardly lion. God wants us to do nothing when we are unsure of the something we should do when a decision needs to be made.

Is there a relationship in your life that you are unsure of? Stand still—do nothing—until God gives you an answer. Are your children making unwise decisions in their lives and you doubt they will return to the Lord? Stand firm in God's promise that if you raise a child in the Lord, when he is old he will not depart from it (Proverbs 22:6). God does not tell us what happens in those "in between" years, so stand on that promise. Perhaps there is a large purchase you want to make and just aren't quite sure if the timing is right; stand firm and give yourself a day or two to allow God to give you an answer.

God will always help us make the right decisions when we stand still and wait for His answer. Some answers take longer than others, but they are always on time. God is never early and never late. Stand still and wait for the perfect answer from the perfect God.

Prayer

Heavenly Father, thank You for all of the right choices I have made through Your guidance. Thank You for loving me so much that You remind me to stand still and wait for Your answer…

November 20

Found by God

"For the eyes of the Lord run to and fro throughout the whole earth, to show Himself strong on behalf of those whose heart is loyal to Him."

—2 Chronicles 16:9

Oh, how I want to be found by God! I want to be one of those whom He has sought out while traveling to and fro around the world. I want His strong support as I completely and willingly live out His plan for my life (Jeremiah 29:11). I want to be the apple of His eye (Deuteronomy 32:10) and the sheep that hears His voice (John 10:4). I want to find shelter under His wings from the storms in my life (Psalm 91:4) and let Him carry my burdens (Psalm 55:22). I want to serve Him with all my heart, soul, and mind (Matthew 22:37). Oh, how I want to be found by God....

Prayer

Precious Lord, how my heart yearns for You! I want to be found by You! Fill me with Your Spirit and perfect my heart as I loyally follow You...

November 21

Living Among Wolves

"Behold, I send you out as sheep in the midst of wolves. Therefore be wise as serpents and harmless as doves."

—Matthew 10:16

Let's face it—we live in a wolves' world. Wolves devour the meek and the mild. Sometime during our Christian walk, you and I will feel the nip of a wolf or two at our heels. But we need not despair; we have resources to help us escape the clutches of those whom the devil has sent to hinder us.

We have God's Word, the Holy Spirit, and prayer to help us ward off the nips of the enemy. We also have our fellow believers to encourage and pray for us. Using these resources can help us become as cunning as a serpent, slithering by the enemy and leaving him hungering for his next meal, all the while maintaining the harmlessness of a dove.

Ask God to fill you with His wisdom, and remember to use those resources He has given you so that you can escape when the wolves come nipping at your heels.

Prayer

Father, thank You for the tools You have given me to ward off the attacks of the enemy. I know that in Your strength I can resist Satan and his temptations. It is through You and the blood of Jesus that I am victorious…

November 22

Revealed to Babes

At that time Jesus answered and said, "I thank You, Father, Lord of heaven and earth, that You have hidden these things from the wise and prudent and have revealed them to babes."

—Matthew 11:25

Have you ever heard the expression "You are too smart for your own good"? Jesus felt that way about the "wise and prudent." He thanked His Father for choosing to reveal His truth to those who were as innocent as babes. Little ones will sit at your feet, looking up at you with puppy dog eyes, and absorb every word you say. They can't wait to run to a friend and say, "My mommy (daddy, grandma, grandpa) said…" They do not question your words or analyze them; they simply accept them as truth.

Jesus wants you and me to be like those excited little children—to be babes in Christ. Don't try to analyze or understand every detail. Accept the understanding He has given to you. When you are ready for a new truth, God will reveal it; He loves to reveal truth to His kids.

Prayer

Lord, please be with those who are taking their baby steps in You. Give them a desire to stay in Your Word and watch for the truth You will reveal to them…

_____
_____
_____
_____
_____
_____

November 23

Safe and Secure

"Or how can one enter a strong man's house and plunder his goods, unless he first binds the strong man? And then he will plunder his house."

—Matthew 12:29

Satan is so sneaky; he knows he can't spoil or rob our spiritual houses unless he first binds us with the stuff of this world. If he can occupy our time with trying to undo the cords of sin and temptation in our lives, he can weaken us. When we become weak, we are ready for plundering.

In order to protect our houses from theft, we need to continually strive to become strong in the Lord and be aware of everything that goes on around us. We need to put on the full armor of God and resist the wiles of the devil (Ephesians 6:11–18). We need to stand firm, using the sword of the Spirit and prayer as our defense. Then God will fight the battle for us and allow us to have victory in our houses.

Are you ready for the next assault, or is your house a prime target for theft?

Prayer

Lord, I love my house, both physically and spiritually. Please remind me to continually be aware of Satan and the temptations he places in front of me. I want my house to be safe and secure in You…

November 24

According to Your Works

"For the Son of Man will come in the glory of His Father with His angels, and then He will reward each according to his works."

—Matthew 16:27

I was scheduled to have surgery for my gallbladder in May 2005. A nurse called me about three weeks before the surgery to tell me it would have to be changed to a different day because the surgeon was overbooked. I asked myself, who decided which patients had priority? Who juggled those schedules to make everything work?

Immediately, I began to think about how I juggle Jesus around in my overbooked schedule. In the course of my day, how much time do I spend serving Him? As I fill in my day planner, do I pencil Jesus in on a page so it can be erased and rescheduled if need be? When my day gets too hectic, is it my devotion time, church, or Bible study that is dropped because everything else is more important? When all is said and done, those things that will have eternal rewards are the things done in the name of Jesus.

Who is in control of scheduling my day? I am. It is up to me to put Jesus first in my life. I will be rewarded according to my works. How will you be rewarded?

Prayer

Precious Savior, You found me so important that You died a horrible death on the cross in order for me to have the greatest reward of all—eternal life. Forgive me for putting unimportant things before You. Please help me to prioritize the plans for my day, putting You first…

November 25

Ready for Jesus

"And while they went to buy, the bridegroom came, and those who were ready went in with him to the wedding; and the door was shut."

—Matthew 25:10

I remember as a child how excited I would get waiting for things to happen. It may have been as simple as waiting for something to come from a catalog order or as exciting as waiting for a phone call from a boyfriend. The waiting was fun until the wait became too long; I would give up the waiting to do something else. Then, without fail, what I was expecting arrived or happened, and I wasn't ready for it.

We, as believers, are waiting for our Bridegroom to come. Jesus doesn't want us to ever give up waiting. He wants us to be like the wise virgins who not only kept their lamps lit; they also kept jars of extra oil ready so they would not be caught off guard. They wanted to be ready when the cry came: "Behold, the bridegroom is coming" (Matthew 25:6); they did not want the door to shut before they could enter the marriage chamber.

Are you ready for Jesus, your Bridegroom, to return?

Prayer

Lord, I want to be ready for You. I do not want to miss out on the best relationship of my life! Thank You for loving me and promising to come back for me…

November 26

A Christmas Bargain

"For where your treasure is, there your heart will be also."

—Matthew 6:21

The Friday after Thanksgiving is traditionally the biggest shopping day of the year—the Christmas shopping bargain kick-off. Personally, you could not pay me enough money to get up with the chickens and wait in line with a mob for the doors to open so that I could get a great sale on anything.

I was watching the news on the evening of November 26, 2004. It was stated that more than 130,000,000 consumers were packing the stores that day. A video clip accompanying the story showed people stampeding one another to get to the "bargain" before it sold out. The shoppers were literally running over each other and walking on the fallen bodies!

What bargain could possibly be worth risking life and limb for? I could think of only one gift that would be worth that risk: the gift of a baby named Jesus and the salvation He freely offers. Sadly, there are many who have their treasures here on earth and not in heaven, and they will all pass away (Matthew 6:19). They do not see the eternal value of God's precious gift of His Son. If only all of those stampeding shoppers had their hearts in the right place....

Prayer

Heavenly Father, thank You for the precious gift of Your one and only Son. He is the bargain of a lifetime, yet many pass Him by. Please help me to share a bargain gift this year—remind me to share Jesus...

November 27

The Wedding Banquet

"For many are called, but few are chosen."

—Matthew 22:14

You and I have been invited to a wedding banquet at the King's palace. Although many of us have been invited, only some will be allowed entry. You see, in order to attend, there is one requirement: we must be wearing the proper clothing. Jesus' garment of salvation is the dress code for the event. We must be clothed in His righteousness. Oh, a few of us might try to sneak into the party in our human apparel, thinking there will be too many people in attendance for the King to notice one person dressed improperly. But the King will notice and ask His servants to take those not wearing a wedding garment and remove them from the banquet (Matthew 22:13).

Do you have on the right garment to attend the King's wedding banquet? If not, take this moment to ask Jesus to forgive you of your sins and to come and live in your heart. Then get ready for that day when you can walk proudly through the doors to a feast prepared just for you.

Prayer

Lord, thank You for finding me worthy of a wedding feast. I can't wait to sit at that table prepared just for me. Thank You for the gift of my wedding garment, which was purchased by the sacrifice of Your Son…

November 28

Easy to Honor

"Honor your father and your mother, that your days may be long upon the land which the Lord your God is giving you."

—Exodus 20:12

As I think about my parents, I realize how blessed I am to have godly parents who are easy to honor. They are easy to honor because they are loving and kind. Mom and Dad have always practiced what they believed and followed up their words with actions. But there are some people who have moms and dads who are not affectionate and far from godly. Are we required to honor them? I believe we are. We do not have to like what they are doing, but we should not bad-mouth them or put them down in front of others.

God thinks it is so important to honor our parents that He attached a promise to His command to honor them: you can live a longer life on this earth. Take a moment right now to pray for your parents if they are still living. Ask God to give you a new way of honoring them.

Prayer

Heavenly Father, I pray right now for the moms and dads who need you. Place someone in their lives who can introduce them to Jesus. When He is in control of our actions, it is easy to become a person to whom honor can be given…

November 29

Model Jesus

"Therefore whatever they tell you to observe, that observe and do, but do not do according to their works; for they say, and do not do."

—Matthew 23:3

All of us have been guilty of not practicing what we preach sometime during our life. How many of us have told our kids not to use "potty talk" and then sounded like a cursing sailor when someone cut us off on the road? Perhaps we have told our kids not to smoke, but when the job got really hectic we stepped outside for a cigarette. Did you remember the two or three beers you drank after work to calm down one day, yet you told your teens not to drink at a party that night?

Moms and dads, we must model the behavior that we expect from our kids! Ask God to show you areas of your life that need to be cleaned up so that your kids see what you want them to become.

Prayer

Jesus, You were the Perfect Model for Your children. Please help me to be the best model I can be for my children and anyone else who watches the way I live my life…

November 30

Truly Committed

But Ruth said: "Entreat me not to leave you, Or to turn back from following after you; For wherever you go, I will go; And wherever you lodge, I will lodge; Your people shall be my people, And your God, my God. Where you die, I will die, And there will I be buried. The Lord do so to me, and more also, If anything but death parts you and me."

—Ruth 1:16–17

As we continue into the twenty-first century, it seems apparent that more and more people do not understand what commitment really means. Couples marry, repeating the words "until death do us part," only to announce their divorce two or three years later. I have several friends who have had many jobs over a five-year period because "it wasn't really what I wanted." On the news this week I heard that United Air Lines has been given permission to not honor their retirees' pensions in order to enable the company to get back on its feet financially. What about all of those men and women who were faithful to United for thirty-plus years? Their pensions may be cut or eliminated. Where is this company's commitment?

If more people lived like Ruth, our entire society would be very different. You see, Ruth understood and lived a life of true commitment. Are you truly committed to keeping your words?

Prayer

Father, please forgive me for the times I have not been truly committed. From this day forward, I want every action I take to back up every word I say. I can only do this through You…

December

December 1

Voice Recognition

Now the Lord came and stood and called as at other times, "Samuel! Samuel!" And Samuel answered, "Speak, for Your servant hears."

—1 Samuel 3:10

What is the first thing most of us do after we have buckled our seat belts and started the car? Turn on the radio or put in a CD. We don't want to be alone on our commute or while we are running errands.

Did you know that Jesus wants us to turn Him on and tune Him in first thing in the morning so we don't have to go through our day alone? As we tune Jesus in at the beginning of our day, He can instruct us in the way we should go. Our ears will be hearing the voice that reminds us to be patient, loving, kind, and forgiving.

You need to be able to recognize God's voice in order for Him to guide you. When God spoke to Samuel during the night, he didn't recognize the voice at first; he had to hear it a few times and be encouraged by Eli to respond to the call. Are you able to recognize and respond when God is speaking to you?

Prayer

Precious Lord, I am so blessed to know Your voice! Thank You for Your guidance in my life; I would be lost without You. When You speak to me, help me to willingly obey Your commands…

December 2

Friend of Jesus

But Jesus said to him, "Friend, why have you come?" Then they came and laid hands on Jesus and took Him.

—Matthew 26:50

According to *Webster's Dictionary*, the definition of friend is "one attached to another by affection or esteem; one that is not hostile; a favored companion."[29] Why then did Jesus call Judas "friend" when he came to betray Him in the Garden of Gethsemane?

As I thought about that question, God gave me an answer: Jesus was known as a friend of sinners (Matthew 11:19), and Judas was a sinner. Jesus died on the cross because He wanted to redeem people like Judas.

You and I are sinners. The only reason we have a hope and a future is because Jesus loved us and died for us "while we were still sinners" (Romans 5:8). If Jesus is your Savior, Lord, and Friend, take time right now to thank Him; if not, ask Him into your life right now. He is waiting…

Prayer

Precious Savior, thank You for dying for me while I was still a sinner. Thank You for calling me "friend." Where would I be without You…

December 3

For This Time

"For if you remain completely silent at this time, relief and deliverance will arise for the Jews from another place, but you and your father's house will perish. Yet who knows whether you have come to the kingdom for such a time as this?"

—Esther 4:14

Queen Esther was one of the most beautiful women in her kingdom (Esther 2:7). But did you know that Esther was FAT? She was faithful, available, and teachable. She was faithful to God, because she approached Him first during three days of fasting and prayer before she approached the king on behalf of her people. Esther was faithful to her people, the Jews. She approached the king on their behalf without being sent for, even though it could have meant her death. Esther was available in the palace to save her people because she listened to the wise counsel of Mordecai and walked in obedience, even as a young girl. Becoming a queen in the king's palace meant that Esther had to learn a new way of life, so she was also teachable.

You and I are called to be FAT people in the kingdom of God. We are to always be ready "for such a time as this" when God gives the call. Are you ready?

Prayer

Lord, thank You for placing me right where I am. I know that I am here "for such a time as this." I pray that I am always faithful, available, and teachable…

_____

_____

_____

_____

_____

_____

December 4

Delivered from Fear

I sought the Lord, and He heard me, And delivered me from all my fears.
—Psalm 34:4

Fear paralyzes—it keeps many of us from attempting to do the seemingly impossible. God always calls the believer to do the impossible; only then can we rest in the assurance that it was God who enabled us to complete our task.

King David had much to fear during his reign. He called on his God, knowing that He would hear, and God was faithful to hear David. God gave David rest and peace when by human standards there should have been neither.

Do not let fear keep you from fulfilling God's calling on your life. He will enable you to do the impossible if you call on Him.

Prayer

Lord, You are the Creator; nothing is impossible for You. Please help me to put my fears to rest as I wait on You...

December 5

In Spite of Fear

Though fear had come upon them because of the people of those countries, they set the altar on its bases; and they offered burnt offerings on it to the Lord, both the morning and evening burnt offerings.

—Ezra 3:3

God loves it when His people step out in obedience in spite of their fear. There will always be something or someone who wants to interfere with our worshipping and obeying God. We can fear the rejection, ridicule, or proverbial stoning by family and friends and hide our worship, or we can love God enough to offer Him the sacrifice of obedience and worship Him openly.

As I write this, I am thinking of several women I know who have unbelieving husbands. They faithfully attend church and Bible studies, even though they know there will be repercussions when they get home. The knowledge that the Holy Spirit will be there to give them comfort and peace gives them the courage to obey God—in spite of fear.

Prayer

Precious Lord, thank You for the privilege of worshipping you openly. There are believers in other countries who are killed for proclaiming Your name. Please help me to step out in obedience even if it means I am persecuted…

December 6

Jesus Is Coming

For the Lord Himself will descend from heaven with a shout, with the voice of an archangel, and with the trumpet of God. And the dead in Christ will rise first. Then we who are alive and remain shall be caught up together with them in the clouds to meet the Lord in the air. And thus we shall always be with the Lord.

—1 Thessalonians 4:16–17

As I sat in my car one afternoon waiting for my husband to run errands, I heard a song on a Christian radio station that made me homesick for heaven! The words "People get ready, Jesus is coming,…" (lyrics by Crystal Lewis) made me close my eyes and picture how awesome that day will be.

I want to be ready—don't you? None of us know when it will happen (Matthew 24:36), but it will take place in the twinkling of an eye (1 Corinthians 15:52). He will come back and snatch us up, and we will be with Him forever.

Prayer

Dear Jesus, I can't wait to see You. I don't know when You are coming, but I will wait as long as it takes—no giving up and no turning back! Thank You for the promise that You will return…

December 7

God's Fingerprints

Then God saw everything that He had made, and indeed it was very good. So the evening and the morning were the sixth day.

—Genesis 1:31

God has touched everything with His mark. You can see the fingerprints of God everywhere you look.

There is a song that I think of as I write this: I Believe (words and music by Irwin Graham, Jimmy Shirl, Ervin M. Drake, and Al Stillman). This song reminds me that the fingerprints of God are in the miracle of birth, the intricate veins of a green leaf, or the collage of colors of fall leaves rustling in the wind on a brisk day. The beautiful hues of pale pink, lavender, and blue in the evening sunset could only have been painted by God. Only a Master Craftsman could have formed the tiny hummingbird, hovering over a tube-shaped flower, wings fluttering so quickly they can't be seen.

Yes, I see the fingerprints of God everywhere—"and indeed it was very good."

Prayer

Father God, You are truly the Lord of Creation. I see Your touch in every area of my life. Thank You for allowing me to see the expression of Your love all around me…

December 8

Published Yet?

Bear one another's burdens, and so fulfill the law of Christ.

—Galatians 6:2

God has blessed me with the gift of words to help others "bear their burdens." Over the past six years, I have written some of my devotions specifically for my friends to encourage them through difficult situations. Many of these friends have asked, "When are you going to get this book published?"

According to the dictionary, the definition of publish is "to make generally known; to issue the work of."[30] God spoke into my heart that I have already been published—published in the hearts of those special people who were touched by a Scripture that took on new meaning for them and by words of encouragement from the insights given to me by God.

Have you been published in the heart of someone lately? Take time this week to help share the burden of someone who is hurting. If you ask Him, God will give you the right words to say.

Prayer

Heavenly Father, thank You for my brothers and sisters in Christ who have helped me carry my burdens over the years. Thank You for the friends I have encouraged through Your words…

December 9

With Integrity

So he shepherded them according to the integrity of his heart, And guided them by the skillfulness of his hands.

—Psalm 78:72

Billy Graham didn't begin life as a respected, world-famous evangelist; he earned that title by living his entire life with integrity. David didn't begin his career in the palace as a king; he became the shepherd of a kingdom only after showing he had cared for his sheep in the field with integrity. God watched how both men lived their lives on a daily basis and found them worthy of promotion.

Whether you are a stay-at-home mom, garbage collector, waitress, secretary, schoolteacher, or CEO of a company, be the best you can be. Maintain your integrity and work "as to the Lord and not to men" (Colossians 3:23). Even if no one else appears to be watching, God is. Serve Him with integrity.

Prayer

Lord, I want to honor You with every word I speak and every action I take. I want others to speak of me as a person of integrity…

December 10

Dabbling in This World

"And after all that has come upon us for our evil deeds and for our great guilt, since You our God have punished us less than our iniquities deserve, and have given us such deliverance as this, should we again break Your commandments, and join in marriage with the people committing these abominations?"

—Ezra 9:13–14

It started with Eve in the Garden of Eden and continues today: We reap what we sow. Satan conned Eve with a cunning twist of words: "You will not surely die" (Genesis 3:4). Adam and Eve broke God's commandment, and they had to pay the price.

I have heard it said, "The eyes are the windows to the soul." Therefore, what we feast on visually—as well as physically and mentally—controls us. When we lust after and give in to the things of this world, we end up paying the price—just as the Israelites did when they disobeyed God. Does God forgive us? You bet He does! But we still have to suffer the consequences of our actions. God's government goes on.

The next time you are tempted to do something ungodly, remember to consider this: What price are you willing to pay just to dip your toes into the waves of this world that are breaking onto the beach of your life?

Prayer

Precious Lord, I do not want to hurt You by dabbling in the things of this world. Please convict me right now of those things that You want to see purged from my life. I want to be a clean vessel for You...

_____

_____

_____

_____

_____

_____

_____

December 11

Everlasting Love

The Lord has appeared of old to me, saying: "Yes, I have loved you with an everlasting love; Therefore with lovingkindness I have drawn you."

—Jeremiah 31:3

Everlasting love: it has no beginning and no end. It is the kind of love only God is capable of giving.

Although there are different types of love, we use the same word to say we love our pets, spouses, homes, children, jobs, churches, and God. Each type of love is unique, but none are everlasting; they are conditional. We fall out of love and dispose of things that once took priority in our lives—even God. But God never falls out of love with us! He even loved us while we were still sinners (Romans 5:8). There is nothing that can separate us from His love (Romans 8:37–39).

Are you basking in the radiance of God's everlasting love? He is only a prayer away.

Prayer

Heavenly Father, thank You for loving me even when I am unlovable. There have been many times when I have disappointed You, but Your arms were always ready to hold me tight with everlasting love…

December 12

Intimate Worship

And when Jesus was in Bethany at the house of Simon the leper, a woman came to Him having an alabaster flask of very costly fragrant oil, and she poured it on His head as He sat at the table.

—Matthew 26:6–7

Have I touched Jesus today? Am I truly worshipping Him in spirit and in truth? What in my life has been poured out for Jesus that is as precious to me as the ointment was in the woman's alabaster flask? Pouring the ointment on Jesus' head was an intimate moment for this woman; she did not care what others thought. She only cared for her Jesus and loved Him with her whole heart.

My own heart grew sad as I thought of those times when I had an opportunity to touch Jesus in an intimate way and missed the chance; the reasons don't matter. What matters is that every believer should feel free to express their love for the Savior in any way they choose, without being concerned about others. We should always feel free to touch Jesus. Have you touched Him today?

Prayer

Precious Lord, I do not want to miss any opportunities to touch You. Please give me a boldness to come before You intimately, without worrying what others think or say. "I am my beloved's, And my beloved is mine" (Song of Solomon 6:3)…

December 13

True Treasure

And He said to them, "Take heed and beware of covetousness, for one's life does not consist in the abundance of the things he possesses."

—Luke 12:15

Christmas greed—we have all been bitten by it, especially children. During the weeks prior to Christmas, I have heard "Nana, I have to have that for Christmas" from all of my grandchildren. Each one could recite word for word all of the commercials for toys. Adults are not exempt from this greed. Television ads convince us that we need much more than we can actually use.

It seems that the world measures success by how much one has or how expensive something is. God warns us to watch where we lay up our treasures (Matthew 6:19), because life consists of more than material things.

Have you found yourself coveting something that you don't really need? Ask God to put things into perspective for you.

Prayer

The goods of this world will pass away, Father. Please help me to remember where true treasure lies. Let me focus my eyes on You and not on the things of the world…

December 14

Full and Overflowing

You prepare a table before me in the presence of my enemies; You anoint my head with oil; My cup runs over.

—Psalm 23:5

There is an old children's song that came to my mind as I was reading Psalm 23 today: "Running over, running over,...."

The life of every believer should be so full of God's love and blessings that it runs over into every area of our life, touching everyone around us. Our overflow should touch those we come into contact with who are hurting, rejected, sick, or alone. We should want them to know that Jesus can be their Shepherd; He restores souls; He walks through sorrows with us, showering us with goodness and mercy. But God gives each of us the choice to have hearts that overflow with His goodness. Have you chosen to let your cup run over with the love of Jesus?

Prayer

Dear Jesus, I come to You right now with the simple faith of a child. Please fill my cup until it runs over and touches everyone around me…

December 15

Youthful Vigor

Remember now your Creator in the days of your youth, Before the difficult days come, And the years draw near when you say, "I have no pleasure in them."

—Ecclesiastes 12:1

There are certain Scriptures in the Bible that have little or no meaning for us until we reach a maturity level where they become applicable in our lives. Until I was in my fifties, I couldn't really appreciate what Ecclesiastes 12:1–5 was saying. These verses tell us to serve the Lord while we are young and have the strength and capability to do anything He calls us to do. As we grow older, parts of our bodies begin to give out. We lose our teeth, our eyesight becomes blurry, and our shoulders become stooped. Some of us become paranoid and are afraid to leave our homes.

It is pretty hard to go about God's work when our equipment breaks down. So, if you are young, get busy for God! If you are in your golden years, don't despair—God's not through with you yet!

Prayer

Lord, thank You for giving me another day to serve You. Let me do so joyfully and earnestly, living each day as if it were my last…

December 16

Incredible Words

"But behold, you will be mute and not able to speak until the day these things take place, because you did not believe my words which will be fulfilled in their own time."

—Luke 1:20

Has God spoken something into your life that seems so incredible that you just can't bring yourself to believe it? Well, you are not alone. In the first chapter of Luke we are told that Zacharias did not believe the words spoken to him by an angel of the Lord, promising him and Elizabeth a son, because they were both past childbearing years. Because of his unbelief, Zacharias was struck dumb and not able to speak until John was born and God's prophecy was fulfilled.

God will fulfill His promise that He has spoken into your life. Don't wait to be struck speechless to believe! Accept His promise; believe He will equip you to fulfill His plan for your life. Then, step out in faith and begin doing the work He has planned for you to do.

Prayer

Lord, Your promises are true. Thank You for the incredible words You speak into my life…

December 17

Perfected Praise

They were indignant and said to Him, "Do You hear what these are saying?" And Jesus said to them, "Yes. Have you never read, 'Out of the mouth of babes and nursing infants You have perfected praise'?"

—Matthew 21:15–16

Children love to be heard. When given the opportunity to perform, they often shout out their parts because they want to be sure they are heard. Kids were the same in Jesus' day. After His entry into Jerusalem on the back of a colt, Jesus went into the temple to shouts of "Hosanna to the son of David!" as the children praised Him. The scribes and chief priests were very unhappy with the loud cries of the children. But instead of asking the little ones to be quiet, as the elders of the church expected, Jesus made it clear that perfect praise would come "out of the mouth of babes and nursing infants" (Matthew 21:16).

You and I are God's children. Our praises should be pure, innocent, and childlike; they should be shouted from the rooftops, as if we were performing for the world.

Are you on stage for Jesus, or are you hiding in the wings, waiting for someone else to shout their praises first?

Prayer

Lord, please give me the purity and boldness of a little child. Only as I come to You as a little one will my faith be perfected. Please help me to be quick to shout Your praises to a world that is ever watchful...

December 18

Jewels in My Crown

Children's children are the crown of old men, And the glory of children is their father.

—Proverbs 17:6

During Christmas 2003, two of my young granddaughters, Zoë and Darian, were in a church pageant entitled "Mission: Possible." This pageant was the Christmas story presented in a contemporary fashion. The choir's robes were "spy gear"—jeans, T-shirts and sunglasses; King Herod even break-danced!

As the story unfolded and I watched my beautiful little treasures singing in the choir, tears began to trickle down my face. I thought, "This is my legacy, God." My treasure was to see my grandchildren being raised in the church, learning to enjoy Him, to serve Him, and to spread the Good News. If I leave nothing else in this world, I know that I have passed on a godly inheritance to my children and grandchildren.

I thanked God in the quietness of my heart as I watched those two little jewels in the crown of my old age helping to spread a mission that is possible—the mission of Jesus Christ!

Prayer

Lord, You have blessed me with six beautiful jewels in my crown. May I never take lightly my duty to always point them to You…

December 19

Carry Me, Daddy

"Even to your old age, I am He, And even to gray hairs I will carry you! I have made, and I will bear; Even I will carry, and will deliver you."

—Isaiah 46:4

What child has not asked the question, "Daddy, will you carry me?" When little legs grow weary and the trek is not over, Daddy is the one who will pick up the straggler, place him or her on his shoulders, and finish the journey.

Our Abba Father wants to do that for His children. He longs for us to ask for His help when we are tiring in our journey here on earth. But most of us are too proud to admit we need help; we try to do everything on our own. It is only when we are broken and can no longer walk or run that we admit we need help.

If you are tired and broken right now, ask your heavenly Daddy to carry you; He will.

Prayer

Abba Father, thank You for the times You have carried me on Your shoulders. When I had no strength left, You became my strength…

December 20

In the Wilderness

So He Himself often withdrew into the wilderness and prayed.

—Luke 5:16

The title of a book on my coffee table, *Just Give Me Jesus*, catches my eye and makes my heart ache. How long has it been since I have been alone with Him? How long has it been since I haven't had the distraction of a phone call, a knock on the door, or an appointment to run to? How long has it been since I've been in the wilderness, just Jesus and me, talking for hours on end? Too long, my heart whispers.

Is your soul crying out for the wasteland? Is your soul crying out for oneness with the Lord? Mine is. What are we waiting for? We are the ones who decide to enter the wilderness; the choice is ours. We can choose Jesus—just Him and a solitary place....

Prayer

Precious Jesus, I choose today to go into the wilderness and fellowship with You. It is in my lonely place that I get to really know who You are. Thank You for the peace that oneness with You brings...

December 21

Changed Lives

"I will give you a new heart and put a new spirit within you; I will take the heart of stone out of your flesh and give you a heart of flesh."

—Ezekiel 36:26

A changed life is great evidence that there is a God. When one sees a once hard, cursing, and cynical tattooed Harley motorcycle rider become the church nursery worker, gently teaching toddlers about how much Jesus loves them, God is at work. The wife who prayed without ceasing for that cynical husband wipes her tears of joy as she witnesses this miracle.

When the hard lines of a set jaw are softened in a once critical young mom's face, God is at work. Peace now etches her face, softening the lines, and love is reflected in her actions as she tends her young children. She and her husband now take them to church to experience what they have experienced—unconditional love. God has been working.

If you take the time to look around, you will see lives changed because God placed within them a new heart—a new life in Christ. Yes, there is a God who is in the business of changing lives. Has He changed yours?

Prayer

Father, thank You for changed lives; thank You for giving us new hearts. I pray that I will always share You freely with others, so they too can experience the miracle of You in their lives…

December 22

God's Requirements

He has shown you, O man, what is good; And what does the Lord require of You But to do justly, To love mercy, And to walk humbly with your God?

—Micah 6:8

God doesn't require much from His children. According to Micah 6:8, we only need to do three things: do justly, love mercy, and walk humbly with God. Easy, right? Wrong! If each of us had to live this way on our own, we would all blow it—especially the humble part.

How many times have you and I had to eat humble pie? Just when we know we have everything down pat, God pulls the rug out from under our feet and knocks the wind out of our sails! But thankfully, God's mercies are new every day; we can pick ourselves up, brush the dust off, and with Jesus and the power of forgiveness walk humbly before our God.

Prayer

Lord, You truly love those who are humble of heart. Thank You for keeping me humble before You. I could not do it on my own; I cannot do it on my own. Thank You for your mercy and grace, which enable me to live a life pleasing to You…

December 23

Trust Jesus

But Simon answered and said to Him, "Master, we have toiled all night and caught nothing; nevertheless at Your word I will let down the net."

—Luke 5:5

Trust Jesus—two words that have the power to change your world; they changed Simon's world. He had fished all night and returned with empty nets. When Jesus told Simon to let down his nets again, he could have argued, but he simply said, and I paraphrase, "We have worked all night and have nothing to show for it, but because You say to, I will let down the net." Simon trusted Jesus. In spite of what he had already experienced, he put his nets back into the water, and they were filled with fish to the point of breaking.

God wants to fill your nets to overflowing. Put your trust in Him. Believe what He speaks into your life; take a step of faith and watch with excitement as your nets begin to overflow with blessings.

Prayer

Lord, when I trust You, I see miracles take place in my life. Thank You for filling my nets with everything I need. Thank You for making me a fisherman in Your Kingdom…

December 24

According to God's Word

Then Mary said, "Behold the maidservant of the Lord! Let it be to me according to your word." And the angel departed from her.

—Luke 1:38

Mary was being given the awesome privilege and responsibility of carrying, birthing, and nurturing the Son of God. She might have asked a lot of questions before accepting this mission for her life, but she asked only one: "How can this be, since I do not know a man?" (Luke 1:34). Mary's response to the angel's answer was short, simple, and from the heart: "I am the Lord's servant." She did not say "Let me think about it" or "Not now; maybe next year." She merely said, "Let it be to me according to your word."

Have you ever given God a "Not now; maybe next year" answer? I did. I procrastinated for six years before completing a work God had given me to do. I missed out on the blessings that could have been mine years earlier if I had only said "I am your servant" and wholeheartedly entered into the work that He had called me to.

Is there a calling on your life that you are putting off because you have too many questions or doubts? Trust God, become His willing and faithful servant, get busy, and joyfully complete the task He has given you.

Prayer

Thank You, Lord, for the awesome opportunity I have to be a part of Your work. Please help me to complete my work joyfully and with purpose. I am Your servant…

December 25

The Perfect Gift

"For there is born to you this day in the city of David a Savior, who is Christ the Lord."

—Luke 2:11

The most perfect gift in the world will not be found beautifully wrapped and placed under a twinkling Christmas tree; the most perfect gift in the world was born in a stable, wrapped in swaddling cloths, and laid in a manger (Luke 2:7), with nothing elegant or sparkling around Him. Baby Jesus came into the world without any Christmas parade, exchanging of gifts, or scrumptious turkey dinner. He did not arrive with any fanfare. But He did arrive to bring the most priceless gift of all—eternal life.

As you spend time celebrating the birth of Jesus this Christmas, think of a gift you can give to Him. It will not have to be wrapped in pretty paper and tied up with a bow; it will have to be something only you can give—yourself.

Prayer

Dear Jesus, thank You for giving me the gift of salvation. This Christmas I want to give myself to You. Please take my life and use it for Your purposes…

December 26

No Fear

Therefore we will not fear, Even though the earth be removed, And though the mountains be carried into the midst of the sea; Though its waters roar and be troubled, Though the mountains shake with its swelling. Selah.

—Psalm 46:2–3

The worst disaster on record so far in my lifetime occurred on December 26, 2004. A 9.0 magnitude earthquake in the Indian Ocean resulted in a tsunami that affected the coasts of eleven countries. At the time of this writing, over 250,000 lives have been lost. More are expected to die from injuries, disease, and exposure to the elements.

How many of those people who died knew the Lord? How many had the peace of God that passes all understanding as those waters roared and crashed over them? If the waves came crashing down around you right now or the earth trembled beneath your feet, could you claim that you would have no fear because the peace of God encompasses you?

Prayer

Lord, You are my peace; You are my firm foundation. Though the world crashes around me, I can stand firm in You…

December 27

I Give You Peace

"Peace I leave with you, My peace I give to you; not as the world gives do I give to you. Let not your heart be troubled, neither let it be afraid."

—John 14:27

It was the morning of my surgery. I opened my daily devotional and read the Scripture for that day. God is so good! He gives us exactly what we need when we need it. Jesus knew I needed Him to be with me and give me peace. He was reminding me in His own words from John 14:27 that there was nothing to fear. My future was in His hands, so I needed only to rest in His peace and trust in the surgeon that God already knew would be operating on me.

You may not be facing surgery, but there might be something in your life that is causing you to fear. Turn it over to Jesus; He will hold your hand and remove the fear from your heart as He goes with you through your turmoil.

Prayer

Precious Lord, thank You for wrapping me in Your peace when the storms of life surround me. You are always there to encourage and comfort, no matter what the situation may be. You truly are my Prince of Peace…

December 28

Healing Will Come

"For if you forgive men their trespasses, your heavenly Father will also forgive you. But if you do not forgive men their trespasses, neither will your Father forgive your trespasses."

—Matthew 6:14–15

Forgiveness does not come easily to the majority of mankind. When someone breaks our heart, hurts a loved one, betrays a trust, or forgets a promise, we want them to feel our pain. But their pain will eventually become ours, because not forgiving others breaks our fellowship with God. How can we who are forgiven much not forgive the sins of our fellow man? God instructs us to forgive in order to be forgiven. Christ died for all of us! Are we more important than a brother or a sister in the Lord or one of our neighbors?

Is forgiveness and compassion toward others easy? Not always. Is it required? You bet! Ask God to give you the strength to forgive those who have hurt you. Healing will come to you as well as to the forgiven.

Prayer

Father, I am so thankful that You have forgiven me of my sin. I ask that You help me to be willing to forgive those who have hurt or betrayed me, passing that forgiveness to them…

December 29

Choose Friends Wisely

Make no friendship with an angry man, And with a furious man do not go, Lest you learn his ways And set a snare for your soul.

—Proverbs 22:24–25

It is very important as a Christian to choose friends wisely. It has been said that we are what we eat, which applies to our spiritual appetite, too. Proverbs 13:20 says, "He who walks with wise men will be wise, But the companion of fools will be destroyed." God wants us to surround ourselves with godly people who have characters we want to emulate.

If you find yourself surrounded by people who are always depressed or angry, you may want to find a new circle of friends. Although we are told that we need to be in the world to witness to the world, our close friends and confidants should be believers. Jesus was a friend of sinners, but His inner circle, the apostles, were godly men.

Ask God to help you evaluate those who are close to you. You may need to enlarge your circle of friends to include wise and godly people.

Prayer

Lord, thank You for the wonderful people You place in my life. It is my desire to surround myself with those who want to grow in You. As this new year is about to begin, help me to choose my friends wisely…

December 30

Boast Not

Let another man praise you, and not your own mouth; A stranger, and not your own lips.

—Proverbs 27:2

Guilty as charged, Lord! So many times over the years I have heard myself singing my own praises. I wanted to make sure that everyone knew my accomplishments and that I got credit for a job well done. Then God convicted me in His Word: "For not he who commends himself is approved, but whom the Lord commends" (2 Corinthians 10:18). I should concentrate on doing God's will, and if any praise comes it should come from someone else.

I had to thank God for reminding me to do the best I can in everything. It doesn't matter if anyone else ever sees what I do—it is all for Him!

Prayer

When pride gets in my way, Lord, please help me to remember Your words and to not sing my own praises…

December 31

A New Song

He has put a new song in my mouth—Praise to our God; Many will see it and fear, And will trust in the Lord.

—Psalm 40:3

God wants everyone to have a new song to sing. Each of us can have a new song when we accept Jesus into our life as our Savior; others hear us singing through our new behavior and it becomes contagious—they want to know where it came from.

A friend of mine once told me she wanted what I had, but she didn't want to give up what I gave up. She saw the song in me, but the thrills of this world, which are temporal, had a strong hold on her. Sadly to say, this friend didn't become a believer. But I don't stop singing, because there are many who still need to come to the Lord. If only one person believes and accepts, it will be worth it all.

As this new year begins, keep singing your song of new life in Jesus. There may be that one person…

Prayer

Lord, thank You for the song in my heart. Please help me to sing loudly for You as this new year begins…

Endnotes

[1] Gordon MacDonald, *Ordering Your Private World* (Nashville, TN: Thomas Nelson Publishers, 1984, 1985, 2003) p. 141.

[2] Beth Moore, *To Live Is Christ* (Nashville, TN: LifeWay Press, 1997) p. 82.

[3] Moore, p. 91.

[4] Henry T. Blakaby and Claude V. King, *Experiencing God* (Nashville, TN: Lifeway Press, 1990) p. 15.

[5] Moore, p. 138.

[6] Misty Bernall *She Said Yes*. Home page, September 29, 2006 <http://www.cassiebernall.com>

[7] Jean L. McKechnie et al., eds., *Webster's New Twentieth Century Dictionary*, 2nd ed. (New York, NY: Simon and Schuster, 1983) s.v. "pleasure."

[8] Chip Ricks, *The Plans of His Heart* (Nashville, TN: Broadman and Holman Publishers, 1996) p. 62.

[9] LDS Mothers Jewish Proverbs. September 30, 2006 <http://www.of-worth.com/ea/mothers.html>>

[10] James Strong, *The New Strong's Exhaustive Concordance of the Bible* (Nashville, TN: Thomas Nelson Publishers, 1990) s.v. "shâchar."

[11] Strong, s.v. "tâmîyd."

[12] Kay Lyons Quotes Database, October 3, 2006 <http://www.laurasmidiheaven.com/Quotes/>

[13] L. B. Cowman, *Streams in the Desert* (Grand Rapids, MI: The Zondervan Corporation, 1997) p. 61.

[14] Corrie ten Boom and John and Elizabeth Sherrill, *The Hiding Place* (Old Tappan, NJ: Bantam Books, 1974) p. 33.

[15] Strong, s.v. "muth_s."

[16] MacDonald, p. 22.

[17] Cowman, p. 443.

[18] Marilyn Hontz, *Listening for God* (Wheaton, IL: Tyndale House Publishers, Inc., 2004) p. 110.

[19] Hontz, p. 109.

[20] Joyce Meyer, *Knowing God Intimately* (New York, NY: Warner Books, Inc., 2003) p. 5.

[21] Meyer, p. 88.

[22] Meyer, p. 201.

[23] Meyer, p. 108.

[24] Meyer, p. 256.

[25] Richard J. Foster, *Celebration of Discipline: The Path to Spiritual Growth* (San Francisco, CA: HarperSanFrancisco, 1978, 1988, 1998) p. 47.

[26] Strong, s.v. "sâmach."

[27] Willy McNamara The Cracked Pot. October 3, 2006. <http://home.att.net~scorch/CrackedPot.html>

[28] Bill Hybels and Mark Mittelberg, *Becoming a Contagious Christian* (Grand Rapids, MI: Zondervan, 1994) p. 92.

[29] McKechnie, s.v. "friend."

[30] McKechnie, s.v. "publish."